# BUTLER'S BIG DANCE

# BUTLER'S

SUSAN S. NEVILLE    Foreword by BOBBY FONG

**INDIANA UNIVERSITY PRESS**
*Bloomington and Indianapolis*

# BIG DANCE

## The Team, the Tournament, and Basketball Fever

This book is a publication of

Indiana University Press
601 North Morton Street
Bloomington, Indiana 47404-3797 USA

iupress.indiana.edu

| Telephone orders | 800-842-6796 |
| Fax orders | 812-855-7931 |
| Orders by e-mail | iuporder@indiana.edu |

∞ The paper used in this publication meets the minimum requirements of the American National Standard for Information Sciences—Permanence of Paper for Printed Library Materials, ANSI Z39.48-1992.

Manufactured in the United States of America

LIBRARY OF CONGRESS CATALOGING-IN-PUBLICATION DATA

Neville, Susan, [date]
Butler's big dance : the team, the tournament,
and basketball fever / Susan S. Neville ; foreword by Bobby Fong.
    p.   cm.
ISBN 978-0-253-22312-8 (pbk. : alk. paper)  1. Butler University—Basketball—History.   2. Butler Bull Dogs (Basketball team)—History.
3. NCAA Basketball Tournament. I. Title.
GV885.43.B88N48 2011
796.323'630977252—dc22

2010035365

1 2 3 4 5 16 15 14 13 12 11

*For my father,*

**JOHN F. SCHAEFER,**

*Butler class of 1949*

To add a page or two
For Butler's fighting crew
Beneath the Hoosier sky.

—FROM "THE BUTLER WAR SONG"

Is that dance slowing in the mind of man?
That made him think the universe could hum?

—FROM "THE DANCE" BY THEODORE ROETHKE

# CONTENTS

## FOREWORD

Sports are the front porch to a university. In the course of the 2010 NCAA Men's Basketball Tournament, Butler University's front porch was crowded. The team entered tournament play with a 28–4 record, including an 18–0 mark in conference play and a championship in the post-season Horizon League Tournament. The Bulldogs, representing a university of 4,500 students, then proceeded to advance to the Sweet Sixteen with wins against University of Texas El Paso and Murray State, to the Final Four with upsets of Syracuse and Kansas State, and to the Championship Game with a victory over favored Michigan State. The team rode a 25-game winning streak into the final against Duke, and the David-vs.-Goliath plot made for a compelling sports story.

But there was more. The Final Four was held in Butler's hometown of Indianapolis, and this enabled the team to attend classes through the week and even on the day of the Championship Game. The men's basketball program had six Academic All-Americans in the last four years, the most basketball players honored of any university, including two on this year's team: Matt Howard and Gordon Hayward. The program not only had high graduation rates among its players, the athletes majored in engineering, math, finance, and education. They were true students, and season practices took place at 6:30 in the morning to accommodate class schedules. People on the front porch looked through the windows of the university in admiration of its academic seriousness.

Susan Neville's book invites you inside the university to share its excitement during this run. She tells the stories and captures the voices of the Butler community, faculty, staff, students, fans, and the team itself. Butler basketball is rooted in a comprehensive campus commitment to excellence in all of our endeavors. Our educational mission is to prepare each graduate not simply to make a living but to make a life of purpose, in which individual flourishing is intertwined with the welfare of others.

May Susan's book help you to experience the heady days of 2010 March Madness at Butler University. I hope it also gives you a sense of the ongoing ethos of our school, which invites you to visit our porch and step through our doors.

BOBBY FONG
*President, Butler University*

# PREFACE
## *On Joy*

This is a book about Butler University's campus and community during the 2010 NCAA men's basketball championship run, and through that lens, it's a book about Indiana's basketball fever and perhaps a book about our longing for heroes. I will try very hard to stay out of this book's way.

It's also a book about joy, that kind of surprising joy that comes in the middle of dailiness, like one of those moments when you look up at the sky and see—out-of nowhere—a multicolored hot air balloon and you give it all your attention and unexpectedly it lifts your heart. It touches something hidden. Where did it come from, you wonder, and why does it touch you so deeply? Beauty does that when it's surprising: an unexpected turn in a poem, the shock of unearned love, the knowledge that human beings can make something good in this world where we make so much that's bad. The knowledge, too, that it's all so ephemeral.

Since everyone I've talked to has asked "why are you writing this book?" (with different emphasis—sometimes on the "why," sometimes on the "you," and sometimes on the "this") and no one seems to be satisfied with any answer I can give, a confession:

Four-year-old Amelia, the girl who lives next door to me, is one of those little girls who always wears dresses. Both her parents are full-time physicians, and her mother lives in hospital scrubs. Her babysitters are young women dressed in the usual jeans and T-shirts, and Amelia has both alternatives to the wardrobe she's chosen and the models for wearing them.

But the dresses are her choice. And the pastel socks she wears with them. She will dress like this, no doubt, until she goes to school and begins dressing the same as her classmates.

Amelia loves baby dolls and the smell of their perfect vinyl skin and the petals of their eyes. She loves pink flowered fabrics and she wears her hair long and curly with barrettes. But none of that holds her back. Her knees are skinned, she flips upside down on the swing set, and she goes so high when she swings on the tree swing that if she were to choose to jump off she would have to grow wings or risk several broken limbs.

When I see Amelia outside running through the grass with her older brother Walker, I think more of a nineteenth-century farm girl working the fields in cotton dresses and reading books by candlelight than I do of, say, a heavily made-up little girl from a beauty pageant. I think of a girl who knows her own mind. Amelia is one of those little girls who loves the feel of the wind on her legs, who loves to twirl in a skirt, who loves the word "pretty." *Why do you always wear a dress?* someone will soon say to her. I know this, or rather I'm imagining it, because this is what people said to me when I was her age. Even then.

So that's why I feel the need to preface this sports book with a confession. Or rather several.

The first I've already implied. My childhood was like Amelia's. I spent my childhood in the world of the prescribed feminine. At some level I knew I had a choice. At some level I felt I might not. That was the era I grew up in. I sewed. I played with dolls. I read Nancy Drew books and Jane Austen, and I've never been an athlete. I don't have a single gift in that direction.

My son played football and baseball through high school. If the weather's nice or there are fireworks, I can watch baseball, but I could never even keep my eye on where my own son was when the movement started on the field in football. My daughter played soccer and softball. I envy her strength and power. My son can throw a spiral harder and farther than anyone short of a professional quarterback. My daughter spent two months in Haiti in 2010, busting rubble with a sledgehammer and pushing the heavy rock in wheelbarrows for the Canadian army to cart away to a landfill. Forgive a mother's pride.

I couldn't lift a sledgehammer. And I went to both my children's games and always brought a book to read. I learned to hide it the way my students hide their instant messaging during classes.

I grew up around men and a few great-aunts talking almost exclusively, and animatedly, about sports. I saw how it bonded them, and I never felt left out. Relieved is more like it. It gave me the space and the freedom to read and write, to think my own thoughts and, as well, to observe pure attention and joy in those I loved. I love, too, how girls who play soccer and basketball in high school seem insulated against some of the craziness of adolescence. I love their muscles and confidence and ferocity, and I love the competitive spirit my women students have, a spirit I think they had less access to when I started teaching. I attribute it to sports. I do.

But until I started writing this book, I never read the sports page. I never participated in the game or in the conversation. I have felt as though it were another language. It was a language I had no facility with or the slightest wish to learn.

And while I'm at it, I might as well say that I absolutely loathe Lucas Oil stadium, the offstage but ever-present setting of much of this story. Lucas Oil has the look of a fieldhouse, but it's not the real thing. It's entirely out of human scale. It hulks. It looms. You can see it from space. I expect it to grow legs at midnight some Halloween and start walking around, like Godzilla, crushing all our churches and schools and museums and sidewalks and our libraries and our trees and flowers and our loved ones into tiny pieces.

Peyton Manning is just fine with me, as were the Edge and Pierre Garcon. All the Colts are just fine with me, in fact. It was cool when we won the Super Bowl. I loved Tony Dungy. But I hate that cathedral we built for them. I doubt that it was built to last for centuries.

Basketball? Well, basketball is another thing entirely.

I was born and grew up in Indiana, and while I don't feel the moves kinetically the way I feel the keys of a typewriter or piano or the strings of a violin or the pages of a book, the language of basketball and the rhythm of the season and the way basketball is woven into the culture are entirely familiar to me.

I know the feel and heft and the color and the taste of a basketball. I know the metallic sound it makes on the asphalt, a different sound than it makes on hardwood. I know the heroic names. *Bobby Plump. Isiah Thomas. The Van Arsdales. Billy Shepherd. Larry Bird. Oscar Robertson. John Wooden. Tony Hinkle.* Even *Bobby Knight.* I went to Butler basketball games in Hinkle Fieldhouse when I was a child. I remember the excitement of the IHSAA boys' basketball tourney, and I attended more sectional and regional and semi-state championships at Hinkle than I can count.

I lived in New Castle, Indiana, when all-American Steve Alford was playing ball in the world's largest high school gymnasium. In fact, of the twelve largest high school gyms in the country all but two of them are in Indiana. Four of those are in the Gary/Elkhart region and most of the others are in the former industrial centers of Anderson, Muncie, Richmond, and New Castle. Large but in scale with the community, they are buildings draped around the true spirit of a place. They mean something to generations. They smell like popcorn and sneakers. They're the pattern for what the large professional stadiums are gesturing toward.

Those years watching high school basketball and then the following years when Indiana University won the national championship taught me about Hoosier hysteria, the whole madness and joy of it.

In New Castle, we lived for Friday and Saturday nights. Kids growing up in Henry County would always, they thought, wear green, and they would always be New Castle Trojans even if they moved to another school district in some holy disaster their parents might visit upon them.

The team was their greatest loyalty, the thing that bound them to their community and to generations of their own families. It was culture-making and perhaps even soul-making. It was, more than anything, community-building in a place that had very little going for it economically.

On Friday nights everyone in the town, a town in the middle of incredible economic bust going back to the middle of the twentieth century, was drawn together in the fieldhouse. Had a fight with your husband or feel distant from your kids or your parents or worried about your job or your falling-down house or your money? Whatever it was, during the game itself you let it all out. The primal scream, the ecstatic release, the sorrow and the joy and the frustrations, all of it let loose in watching the boys who were part of you, the best part of you, and whether they won or lost and, even more important, *how* they won or lost was part of you. There were rituals and people playing their roles—popcorn vendor, parent of a player, parent of a player's girlfriend, sister of a friend of a friend, neighbor, and so on—and the whole thing was as cathartic and spiritual as religion and art are supposed to be but often aren't. So I suppose that was a confession too.

At the end of the game you hugged strangers who were no longer strangers. You made up with your spouse or children. And then you talked about the game over breakfast on Saturday. You recalled players who had been dead for years, their signature moves on the court. You talked about ones who were coming up and would soon be playing for you. Myths were created. Steve Alford, it was said, would start every single day shooting free throws and he wouldn't stop until he'd sunk a hundred straight. If he reached 99 and missed the 100th shot, he would begin again at the beginning.

It's not that different, finally, from the repetitive nature of the assembly line at the Chrysler plant where you work, or the fields you plow or the cars streaming by your window at the drive-through. The basketball players lift all that tedium for you and give it to the gods as an offering. Odysseus began his career like that, you know. He was a farmer.

My friend the writer Barb Shoup grew up in Hammond, Indiana. She remembers a woman who had on a vinyl LP the radio broadcast of the game when East Chicago Washington High School won the state championship. Throughout her life, she played the record as she cleaned the house and the joy still lifted her beyond the drudgery.

I understand that. After living in New Castle for five years, we named our firstborn Steven. That's how much I have loved amateur basketball.

But I have never in all my years seen or felt anything quite like the Butler University campus the spring our men's basketball team made it to the Final Four at Lucas Oil Stadium and missed winning the national championship by two points.

As an Indiana writer, Hoosier hysteria has always fascinated me. Why basketball? Why Indiana? And what, finally, is the hysteria? Why does basketball seem to generate such loyalty and such mythology? And what does it feel like when you're a fan caught inside the storm?

When asked to recall their favorite memories about the tournament, most of the 600-some respondents to a Butler survey used words like *electric* and *surreal*. Almost all said they hoped they would never forget what it felt like. When the student journalists who covered the game were called by their counterparts at other schools the primary question was "What is it like on campus?"

And what could you say? It was like nothing else. The story of the 2010 NCAA men's basketball championship season and of the final championship game pitting Butler against Duke a few miles away from their home court in Indianapolis is a mythopoeic story. The book about the games, the schools, the players and strategies will be written. It will be filled with statistics and analysis and stories remembered through the fog of time and distance. And I will read that book and I will keep it on my bookshelf, and I hope it's a good book. What I would like to get at here is what it felt like to be an alum or a parent or, as time went on, a neighbor or a member of the community. The story of the small school making its way through the tournament was both universal and particularly Hoosier, and it happened at a time when perhaps the country itself needed the story.

What I would like to capture right now—because it's rare and ephemeral (even now changing, being revised, being calcified into history)—was the way the tournament was a center of energy that caused a small community

to feel glittery and surreal and important and oddly, at times, almost disconnected from reality.

It's the way it probably felt in Milan, Indiana, in 1954 when a school of 161
students won the state basketball championship by Bobby Plump's two points
against Muncie Central and 40,000 people showed up to celebrate the win. It
was like the moment East Chicago Washington gave a housewife in Hammond
a gift, or like moments during the summer that huge glittery comet Hale-Bopp
hung so quietly in the skies, bringing our attention back to it over and over as
something miraculous. And then forgotten.

Any work of art, any culturally made artifact in this world, is an attempt,
as Willa Cather wrote, to "make a mold in which to imprison for a moment
the shining elusive element which is life itself—life hurrying past us and running away, too strong to stop, too sweet to lose." So here's an attempt—a few
words, some interviews, some quotations, some images—to catch that time
in a bottle, that lightning in a jar—before it fades into history.

# ACKNOWLEDGMENTS

I owe a debt of thanks to so many who helped with this book. The first is my editor at Indiana University Press, Linda Oblack, who responded to an e-mail of mine by saying, "Hey, why don't you write a book about it?" The second is my husband, Ken, who put up with my basketball questions and general spaciness during the marathon writing of the book, who read early drafts, and who encouraged me to lead with my heart. The third is my research assistant, R. Jordan Fischer, a terrific interviewer and journalist who conducted many of the student interviews.

And I want to thank Geoff Sharpless, East Coaster by birth, who helped this native Hoosier see the game with fresh eyes. And my friends Marianne Boruch and Barbara Shoup for their support during the writing. I want to thank Peter Froehlich of Indiana University Press and Susanna Sturgis, an incredible copy editor. I thank the faculty members who took time to be interviewed, including Jon Sorenson, Stephen Laurent, Brynnar Swenson, Robert Pribush, Judith Lysaker, Shelly Furuness, and Brian Murphy. Thanks to Judith Cebula of the Center for Faith and Vocation at Butler University for always asking the right questions and to Pam Hopkins, the Bulldogs' greatest fan.

Thanks to the bookstore staff. And thanks to Ashley Cerda, Caitlin O'Rourke, Emily Newell, Emily Robinson, Erin Cochard, Hailie Davila, Josh Downing, Kevin Masterson, Mackenzie Szmanski, Megan Walker, Sarah Murrell, and the Smith family for taking time to be interviewed. If your words aren't included, they've informed every line.

Thanks to former Butler president Geoff Bannister and to Barry Collier, Thad Matta and to the Lickliters for picking up the strand of Tony Hinkle–style Butler basketball a few years back. Thanks to the Fongs for your support. Thanks to the team and coaches for the incredible ride. Thanks to my good friends Garry and Debbie Barth and Dan Weitz for watching the games with Ken and me and getting us through the excitement.

I also want to thank the students in my senior writing seminar. While the basketball team was playing in the tournament, these students produced work that was also inspirational, including the honors theses by Betsy Shirley, Samantha Atkins, and Amy Kellough that I was privileged to read. I was struck by how much these students' work was influenced by the work of Butler students who came before them. Excellence in any field is always both a delight and a surprise as well as a part of a conversation going back through time.

# BUTLER'S BIG DANCE

## ON FIRE

At two o'clock on the afternoon of the 2010 NCAA men's basketball championship game, Butler University students were for the most part attending class. Anyone would have understood if they'd taken the day off.

Outside the window of the third floor seminar room in Jordan Hall, there were helicopters hovering, all the Bradford pear trees had chosen that day to bloom, one of the fraternities had brought out tricycles and had taken over the sidewalks, and the media was trying to interview anything that moved.

Inside Jordan Hall, students sat with their backpacks and their laptops, their books and their Final Four T-shirts, and they knew they were expected to be doing something different from what they were doing, which is to say, what they always did on a Monday afternoon. You're only young once and it's spring on an idyllic midwestern college campus and it feels like suddenly all the world's attention has descended on you. It feels that way because it has.

Even the team members were in class that day. All day long, when a basketball player emerged from Jordan Hall or Fairbanks or Gallahue, from calculus or history, he would be applauded by the groups of visitors who walked around with shopping bags of Butler merchandise (T-shirts, decals, mugs, pennants, stuffed animals, and so on) or by the faculty and staff sitting on benches between appointments. But the players and their fellow students were trying very hard to stay sane.

The reporters keep asking us why we're here, one student said, when we should be doing something else. Like what? I've come to class, the student said, because if I didn't I feel like I'd just fly away. It's too unreal out there.

"Out there" was the Butler campus. For two weeks, since Butler made it into the Elite Eight, the campus had felt like this. It had started to feel like a movie set, and we were all extras.

You couldn't make your way through the bookstore to get to the cafeteria because it was filled with people buying Butler gear or asking to have their picture taken with you, a real Butler person. Every morning for two weeks there had been at least one radio station broadcasting from the quad, asking students to stop and sing the Butler War Song on their way to class. One of them, an alum who was now a radio personality, was outside my office window every morning while I graded papers. Sometimes I'd crank open the casement windows and just watch him work, remembering when his name was Dave, not Gunner. You've come back! I wanted to shout down to him. It was giddy. It was fun. Each day had become a celebration.

Even Blue, the drooling sometimes snappish bulldog mascot who comes to work each day with his owner, Butler's director of giving Michael Kaltenmark, had become a celebrity. Whenever the players went onto the floor, they had to touch his head for luck and at the same time keep their hands from getting bitten. No matter. There's Blue! Blue, the dog we remember throwing up in the aisles at a Sweet 16 game three years ago because he'd eaten too much popcorn, now had as much personality and color as any cartoon dog. He had a birthday party at Starbucks. He spent a day at a spa. Blue was suddenly a star. Wherever he went, there were cameras snapping.

This morning I woke up, one student said, and there was a camera crew filming the Butler sign in my bedroom window. Another student had seen Mr. Peanut with a film crew at a fraternity house. A barista had learned to draw a bulldog in the foam on top of a latte, another student said, and people were waiting in line for fifteen minutes to get one and then taking a picture of the foam.

The camera-toting pilgrims to the campus, both tourists and members of the media, seemed awe-struck. That was the oddest and most moving thing about it. Some of the visitors—most of them, in fact—were almost worshipful of the place itself. It was as if it were the first time they'd seen a student or a flowering tree, a book, a T-shirt, a computer, a professor, a library, a fountain shaped like a star. They started arriving out of nowhere, it seemed, by car and bicycle and on foot. Some of them seemed to have just appeared out of some other time period, some other century. They brought their children and the children were quiet, as if they were in a church or a museum or on a tour of some national treasure. It was like one of those scenes in a movie where groups of people start arriving at the scene of a miracle. You could tell they were walking through some radiant dream of college. They seemed, oddly, like sleepwalkers. "Some of them seemed in shock," one of my students said later. She was a tour guide for families considering Butler. "It was hard to get them out of Hinkle Fieldhouse," she said. "It was like they were trying to reconcile the place with the movie, or with old black-and-white photos in some album, or with their memories.

"Children would stand in front of the basketball picture in Hinkle and just stare at it, or they'd stand on the court and look up and spin in circles."

The visitors to campus moved from one building to another: the white library that looks like a wedding cake, the high modernist auditorium, the gardens, the greenhouse, the planetarium with its domed eye that opens on the brightest of days.

There are students playing golf with tennis balls! On the day of the championship game, a foursome dressed in preppy shorts and Butler T-shirts was playing campus golf (tee off at the statue of the hands holding the book, etc.) as seriously and quietly as though they were in Augusta.

All the beautiful fountains on campus were flowing with blue water. There was an arch of blue and white balloons at the entrance to the library and a giant blow-up bulldog at the entrance to Butler Way, and every single solitary human being associated with the school was wearing school colors. And students were throwing Frisbees just like you see in movies! Students reading books on the green grass! It was a perfect spring day, and everyone, everywhere, was smiling.

And, too, there were the misty-eyed old men who walked across the campus, some of them with walkers and oxygen tanks, some of them tall and straight-backed but fading, ghostlike, making their way to Hinkle Fieldhouse, that legendary place, as though it were the gates to heaven. They spoke to one another in hushed tones. This was, you could tell, an event they'd been waiting for their entire lives. It took your breath away to see them, it really did. You knew which ones had played basketball years ago. You knew they had to make this pilgrimage.

It was the at-times quiet awestruck attention of the visitors that felt most surreal, the hush of it all.

One of the creative writing students in the seminar room was a young woman who'd been in recovery for three years and who said that right after class she was going to the Center for Faith and Vocation's meditation room to meditate until the game because the "weird energy" was freaking her out. She was afraid she'd lose her sobriety. An honors student, she was working on a spiritual autobiography. As long as I'd known her, she'd seemed an old soul, capable of transcending whatever unreal thing was going on around her. This day was something different.

There were several students in the class working on science fiction novels and several on memoirs and none of it—either the fantasy or the real life—could keep our attention from the world outside the window. But we tried. We did our best. Stay in the moment, we said to ourselves. We were giddy and silly, but we brought our backpacks and our papers and we brought our best game.

Still, there was something so seductive about the sudden eruption of energy that the game gave the campus. You had to love it and appreciate how wonderful it was, but you also had to remind yourself that there was a real world underneath it and that you weren't really living in a fairy tale. In a writing class we write tales. We don't find ourselves living in them. But there we were. You wanted to enjoy the fairy tale while trying your best to hold on to the life you knew would resume the next day, no matter the outcome of the final game. You felt there was a danger you might get stuck in Oz, one student said. The feeling on campus was like a wedding, but an extremely large wedding where all the student and faculty and staff and alumni were the wedding party, perhaps a bit stunned by it all, perhaps a bit too young and unprepared. In an odd way it was like looking at the pictures of a wedding through the patina and silence of something remembered.

But not that. *You are on fire and we are on fire with you,* one of the students wrote. *Until now I thought my father's television outbursts were indicative of a certain psychosis that I could never have access to. My "Hoosierness" was always distant, disconnected from the rest of me. Basketball felt as familiar to me as cricket or camel races . . . But the fever grew, it spread to me, and I was, and am consumed.* She wrote this and could read it with either sincerity or irony, and we weren't quite sure which one she meant or how it should be received. The tone depended on whether she read the sentences to you during the two weeks of the tournament or right after.

Because those two weeks were more than anything a respite from cynicism and even from irony.

She was right when she said we were on fire. We could feel it but had no idea what it meant or why it had descended. It was the complete and utter impossibility of it. Butler University in the Final Four? We just held on and tried to do it well. The day of the championship game was one of those time-stops-sudden-eruption-of-meaning days, those historical moments when something threatens to pull everything into it and renew or destroy it. It might have occurred to you, on that particular day, how something can happen in the world that sends shock waves through a community until you feel like you're part of a story, some sort of narrative that's as unpredictable yet essential as food. A narrative you've been waiting to erupt again for half a century or more.

We could easily have worshipped those boys on the team and their blue-eyed coach. We didn't, because we knew them well before the gods descended. But we still could. Worship them.

What do you do when the gods descend without warning? You put one foot in front of the other and meet your responsibilities. And then you take pictures of yourself in the hallway with a girl who had given herself over to the joy and painted her face with blue paws.

Oh come on, you're saying if you've read this far. It was just a game.

## THE SUMMIT

The night of the 2010 NCAA men's basketball tournament when Butler University made it to the Final Four, when all the media was on campus, you could see the print reporters in suits with their reporter notebooks in Hinkle, taking down impressions; it was hard to walk in any direction without seeing the insect eyes of single television cameras and the snappily dressed on-camera talent. All the cameras and the eyes, both human and glass, were directed at the campus, and we were divided into two parts: basketball players and fans.

Which was essentially true, for those two weeks. And that was the beauty of that time, that rare communal sense.

But the campus could be divided in other ways, including into colleges: liberal arts and sciences, pharmacy, business, education, and fine arts.

Suzanne Fong, a lawyer and the wife of President Bobby Fong, said she wished that basketball could be a knothole into other parts of the university. And so when the presidents of Duke and Butler sat together in Bobby Fong's office before the game, the conversation between the two former English majors turned to comparable areas of excellence, including, in Butler's case, dance.

And so there was the article about the meeting in the April 5 issue of the *New York Times*. And dance got its moment of basketball fame.

In the article, William Rhoden talks about the meeting between the two (did I say "former English major"?) presidents, Bobby Fong and Richard Brodhead, in Fong's office the afternoon of the final game.

"You and I made the same choices with our lives," Brodhead is quoted as saying to Fong. "In college, we decided we would pursue the same subjects; we both went on to graduate school in the same field. Then both of us gravitated to teaching and turned our love of teaching into a different kind of job. You are the head of one school. I'm the head of another school, and we sit across the table as friendly rivals because tonight we'll have this great contest."

The game was on.

---

Why did football bring me so to life? I can't say precisely. Part of it was my feeling that football was an island of directness in a world of circumspection. In football a man was asked to do a difficult and brutal job, and he either did it or got out. There was nothing rhetorical or vague about it. I chose to believe that it was not unlike the jobs which all men, in some sunnier past, had been called upon to do. It smacked of something old, something traditional, something unclouded by legerdemain and subterfuge. It had that kind of power over me, drawing me back with the force of something known, scarcely remembered, elusive as integrity—perhaps it was no more than the force of a forgotten childhood. Whatever it was, I gave myself up to the Giants utterly.

The recompense I gained was the feeling of being alive.

—FRED EXLEY, *A FAN'S NOTES*

---

## THE BOOKSTORE

The 2010 men's championship tournament, when Butler made it to the Final Four, was on Easter weekend. It was spring, there were blooming trees and colored eggs and chocolate, and for the first Easter Sunday in its history, the Sunday between the Michigan State game (Saturday) and the Duke game (Monday), the bookstore was open.

One student came to work that morning straight from church, wearing pearls and a beaded sweater. She had painted her nails blue. After an hour at work she went into the back to change out of the sweater and into a T-shirt because it was so crowded and hot that day in the store.

"We sold over two thousand shirts that Sunday," she said. Everyone who came to campus during the tournament eventually made it to the bookstore in Atherton Union.

At times, during the two weeks between the Syracuse game and the Duke game, there were twenty-five people working at once. "It was madness when we made it to the Sweet 16, but we'd done that before," the manager said. "It really started with the Elite Eight, the real madness."

On Easter morning, when the young woman in the beaded sweater and blue painted nails opened the door, an NBC news crew was waiting for her, and there were over two hundred people standing in line outside the door.

They sold the championship game T-shirts right out of the boxes. They were still hot from the printer.

Who was buying them? People from the neighborhood, families with babies, alums, students, and a lot of people on road trips, passing through Indianapolis from other states and stopping at the Butler campus.

The young woman in the beaded sweater saw some friends from her high school on a college visit, but there wasn't enough time to talk. Everyone was excited and everyone wanted a shirt. That was everyone's ticket into the club. "Now that it's over," the bookstore employee said later, "I've been in a lot more conversations about the excitement, what it was like, but it's hard to explain it."

It's hard to recapture what it was like. The campus radiated energy and noise as well as a freakish calm, all at the same time. "There was a madness that consumed the campus," one student said.

"The way the place went crazy when we beat Michigan State to make it to the final game was one of the coolest moments of my life," said another.

"Seeing my eleven-year-old son on the big screen at Lucas Oil, proudly waving a Butler flag," that was the best moment, said one faculty member. "Taking my kids to Hinkle for the viewing party," said another, "and feeling like my work and my family life were part of one thing, and that thing was good."

"Listening to 72,000 people chanting 'defense' in unison for Butler. Most of all the series of memories of how well the team represented the university, town, and state": that was the best moment for one staff member.

"The whole beautiful run was the constant feeling of joy, excitement, nervous anticipation, and pride that engulfed and buoyed each of us. We were all uplifted by the fever," another recalled.

"It was an extended celebration," President Fong explained, "and the hours were long. By the end, most of us were just running on adrenaline."

You wanted a uniform yourself, something that said you were from Butler. Every student and almost every staff and faculty member wore a Butler T-shirt during the final week. That in itself, the way it wasn't scripted but just happened, was surreal. Every visitor to campus took away bags of them. When you waited in line at the bookstore, you'd be standing next to your dean or a philosophy professor or a student from your class, or next to a friend or neighbor you hadn't seen in years. Parents of children in the local grade schools and preschools came to the bookstore to buy a bit of blue for their kids to wear to school. "Our Bulldogs," said bulletin boards in the Meridian Street United Methodist Church Preschool, and bulletin boards in the cafeteria at the International School. *Our Bulldogs.*

The week before the championship weekend, I saw students who'd graduated from almost all the years I'd been teaching, standing in line together as though time had all along been nothing but an illusion.

There was long-haired Jason from three years ago, his hair cut short now for his job. And Laura, the resident assistant who had run for homecoming queen and written about it, and former students with familiar faces and their own children, all in line with students from this semester.

And there were students from way before my time, middle-aged men and men in their seventies and eighties, men who wanted to tell you what it had been like returning to Indianapolis, and to Butler, after World War II, or after the Korean War or Vietnam. They wanted to talk about what it had been like to fly in their planes over Germany in 1944, what it was like to be based in Italy and then to come back here to this idyllic place where all the girls had been waiting for them, to join a fraternity and play poker and drink whiskey and take classes in accounting and literature and then to get married and have children who came to Butler, as did their children's children. They wanted to talk again about reading Milton in a foxhole in Korea, the way the words changed them, about the teachers who helped them express that change.

The old men walked out into the spring of 2010. The pear trees were blooming and some of the crab apple trees, and some of the white petals were falling on the sidewalks, blowing in the open classroom windows, or landing in their hair as they walked on the sidewalks, like ticker tape.

It was as if there was no such thing as graduation. It was as if we had all been resurrected and were together in one place, this bit of heaven in the heart of the heart of the heart of the country where no one grew old or died or ever grew tired or discouraged because there were young people who lifted your heart and carried it for you.

We went to the bookstore to buy holy relics. We went into the bookstore to remember the past. No matter how cynical we had been the week before, no matter how hopeless we'd felt, no matter if we were basketball fans or not, no matter if we were Republicans or Democrats or American or Korean or Chinese or French, no matter if we were Hoosiers by birth or by choice or kicking-and-screaming-all-the-way fate, no matter if we were the president of the university crowd-surfing on students' shoulders after a victory, or a world-renowned professor of religion working on a book during the game or an after-hours emptier of wastebaskets or a food service worker swiping meal card after meal card all day long, we were all for one week one body.

## T-SHIRTS

And we all wanted shirts, no matter what percentage they took from our weekly paycheck. When we reached the Final Four, there were several designs to choose from, including the popular Final Four logo with the outline of a hand burned into the center of the letters. We got a Sweet 16 shirt and then a Final Four shirt and often another. We knew, all of us, when the bookstore ran out of shirts and when new ones were coming in. "This afternoon at 2:30!" we would shout, and at 2:30 we'd be there in the lines. The Follett bookstore workers were bused in from all over the state and from neighboring states. One would be unpacking the boxes and another stocking the temporary metal shelves. A woman stood by the shelves of small and medium and a man by the shelves of large to XXL. The stacks were four to five shelves high, and there were stacks of unpacked boxes behind the shelves. I need two larges, you would say, and then you would remember a niece or nephew or a friend and you'd add a medium and, what the heck, throw in a small like an extra Christmas gift in case you needed it.

The woman who runs the mailroom in Jordan Hall spent days shipping out boxes of T-shirts to people all over the world. They have to be there by the weekend, someone would say, and spend half a week's salary on the shipping fee. It didn't matter! Someone somewhere needed the relic, a bit of the magic for himself.

Beginning with the navy Sweet 16 shirts, Nike sent different designs to the bookstore, and while at first they looked like Butler shirts as the days went on they began to look a bit, well, Nike-esque, a bit corporate. Unlike the underground T-shirts that showed up at Sigma Chi, which were more personal and had funny sayings *(Matt Howard: Fear the Beard!)* that let you know the person who had designed them knew the school, the Nike shirts were more impersonal. The Final Four T-shirts were gray or white with "Final Four" appearing twice, at one point streaming like a race car, and the word "Indianapolis" and the black and white checks of the Indy 500 flag and a bit of orange with a seam that looks like a basketball. All of these graphics were bigger than the Bulldog or the name of the team (*"Butler Bulldogs,"* the shirt whispers underneath the racing letters of "Final Four"). The name of the school was the one part of the design that the graphic artist left to fate or to luck or skill. You look at that T-shirt and realize it could have been some other team's name. It could have been any team. And that was the wonderful thing about it: the absolute and utter surprise that our name was printed on the shirt.

Though why should it have been a surprise? In some ways it wasn't. The team was undefeated in conference play. They had great players, a great coach. They'd been ranked all season. They'd played like they couldn't lose. The surprise wasn't that they won, exactly; it was that they had won and would be playing *here,* in their own city. Butler is a small urban school. We're used to being under the radar.

But no matter. Now we weren't invisible, and when the T-shirt whose design was meant for anyone was on a Butler student, it became a Butler shirt. It was forgiven all its corporate sins.

For $35 you could buy a print of a cheering crowd (Hinkle Fieldhouse? Lucas Oil Stadium? Not quite either) with Bulldogs printed over it, or for $8.95 a drinking glass. For $20 a Race to the Finish poster, for $8.95 a magnetic decal, for $6.95 a medium foam basketball. As the weeks went by the Nike swish became more prominent.

Even Blue, the bulldog mascot, wore a T-shirt with a Nike swish out on the floor at Lucas Oil. It was cute on the bulldog the way a small pair of branded tennis shoes are cute on a toddler. Little Nikes! Little Reeboks! A little Coach purse, a North Face jacket.

I bought a Bulldog pin and immediately and almost instinctively covered the swish with it. This tournament was not about any corporation. It was not about anything outsized or anything that could be bought. It wasn't about neon-colored Gatorade sweat or about absurd spectacles at halftime.

It was, I realize now, the brand's attempt to redeem itself. It's impossible to separate the tournament from the other athletic events of the spring of 2010.

Tiger Woods, that sweet-faced golfer, the athletic face of Nike, had fallen as all our heroes seemed to fall, and now here was the swoosh flying away from the coasts and the world stage and landing in the middle of our party, which was—and we were aware of this even as we were living in the middle of it—about everything in the world that Nike was not.

## WHY BASKETBALL?

With enough practice and love and some athletic talent, any small town can pull together a team of five boys or girls from those scattered farmhouses. You would think perhaps that a sport of one—tennis or running—would be the choice. But we lack the hills of Kenya and the wealth associated with tennis, and basketball doesn't rely on that one brilliant player. It's the community that matters, the team. And that we can do. We smile when we don't have to in the Midwest, not because we're hiding things (though sometimes we are) but because we've been raised to believe that the other person means well. So we can put together a team. It's truly something good about us. It is.

We've believed there was something pure about this game.

## BENEATH THE HOOSIER SKY

I look at the poster for the film *Hoosiers* and it seriously brings tears to my eyes. I know it's not real. It's the iconic image of the lawn-green fields cut into perfect squares with that one straw-colored square to the right. They're too manicured, those fields, but it's a perfect abstraction of a particular dream of Eden: Indiana, all horizontal fertile planes. Yes, during spring growing season it sometimes feels that green, and yes, those perfect rows and those perfect corners feel like midsummer cornfields and the one straw-colored square is the color of the field corn in autumn when it turns that whitish gold with the gray tarnish, right before it's cut and rolled into bales that shine like silver.

And there's that white farmhouse on the far horizon. If we lived there, we think, we would never be unhappy.

In the foreground of the poster, there's the vertical pole of the basketball goal just hinted at; the hoop is not in the frame because to the boy who left his black and white basketball shoes untied at its base it is, of course, something to be worshipped and the shoes are left as sacrifices and the hoop itself is taller than the sky. The boy has left—gone inside the farmhouse to eat, to the barn or the city to work, to the college to earn a degree, away from his mother and his father and off to the person he will marry, to his children, to his job at the factory or in the office cubicle, to his death, to his eventual sad and tragic death—the boy has left his shoes untied at the base of the goal, but the shoes promise that he will return forever and ever and the shoes will be worn by his sons and by their sons. His Cinderella shoes. Someone will step into them and when that someone does he will return to the square of asphalt which echoes the fields and which his father poured for him one summer.

The father who was once a boy lives in the farmhouse. He had a sister who also lived in the farmhouse.

She moved to New York when she was a young woman. For a brief time she sang in the opera. She flew on private planes and wrote a book. For a while she studied law but never practiced. She lived in a house by the ocean but close to the city. No one understands quite where she got her money but for a time she appeared to have a lot of it.

The father who was once the boy, the one who lives in the farmhouse that belonged to the parents, returned to the farmhouse after World War II. He had spent the war dreaming about those fields and how the grass smelled when it was first cut in the spring and how he would sometimes lie in the lawn outside his house and just stare for hours at the cottonwood seeds that flew from the river and looked like sparks against the sky floating so high and dreamlike up there against the blue, as high as any plane. When the white seeds fell to the ground they would drift down like thick flakes of snow and rest where they fell.

He had been a tail gunner, chosen for the job because he was the shortest boy in the crew. He was eighteen years old when he flew all those missions.

His sister was older. She studied during the war. She took lessons. She moved away. He stayed. He was the one who stayed.

He took care of his parents as they aged. He worked with his hands. He married. He had two children. On Sundays, his parents would talk about the sister who was on the coast, and he knew it was because they could see him that they didn't worry about him. He was a good man. There was never any question of his being a good man.

Perhaps not quite as smart as the sister who left? If he were as smart, he would have been called to the coasts. If he were smart, he would have more money now. He would live in a bigger house. If he were smart, he wouldn't be invisible. If he were smart, he would be more than this thing that you would expect him to be. Even here. In this paragraph.

Every day in the world he's reminded of the coasts. Every news bulletin, every television show, every piece of music, every book, every iota of culture comes from someplace else and asks him to contribute to its existence.

If he were smart, he would get damn sick of it.

And sometimes he does.

He knows that when the world flies over him, they see only squares of green and they wonder how could anyone possibly live there, right here where he lives.

When his parents died, he bought out his sister's share of the farm. That's when he discovered that his parents had been supporting her all through her adult life.

So he lent his sister money, as his parents had done all through their lives and as he will continue to do as long as he's able. It's expensive living out there.

It's hard to keep your moral compass.

He knows there are meth labs in French Lick and New Harmony.

It's hard to keep your moral compass.

When he was a boy, he tested higher on the standardized tests than any of his classmates. He knew that. He had chosen to come back here. It had been a choice, and he had no illusions about it. It's no Eden.

Humility is the highest virtue. He's not sure where he learned that. If they don't notice you when they fly over, you don't stand up and point at yourself. That makes you stupid in the eyes of those who are flying over, the fact that you don't point at yourself. But pointing at yourself would make you stupid in your own eyes.

He worked in a factory. The farm was no longer a working farm, but he lived in the farmhouse. He coached basketball like his father had coached him.

He had stayed. He had chosen to stay. He loved this place and no one could seem to understand why. Not for what it's become necessarily, but for something else. So your kids are moving away? his sister would say to him. Good! Not rooted like you. What is it you're so afraid of?

So deeply rooted. Roots grow underneath the soil. It's plants that are rooted. Farmers that are rooted. It's not lack of imagination. Predators run because of hunger, not imagination. Prey run because of fear, not imagination.

He's not one to run. He goes down deep. He remains hidden. That's the way it is.

Their father built the square of asphalt next to the field. It echoes the flatness of the land and it echoes the geometry. He watched his children run up and down and up and down the asphalt in the same motion the farmers used to plow and harvest the fields. The repetition, the hard work. The hundreds of attempts at getting the angle right before you score.

And maybe one day someone will be watching when you get it absolutely right, the long three-pointer. Or maybe no one will notice it at all. But you'll know you made it.

And if someone notices and remembers, it will be something that you did with a team. Five of you, that's all it takes, from one square of township. Just five. It's possible to do that. And you can be tall and a center or you can be short and run and shoot from the outside if you have enough heart, if you've practiced enough on the asphalt in the middle of the field.

Either way.

And there's always the possibility of heroic action, and as long as you live people will speak your name with something like reverence as part of the team that won. The team.

## TOWARD A THEORY OF INDIANA BASKETBALL

It was early in the tournament, "too early for me to think about canceling or shortening my night class. I didn't think we would win. And I didn't get it quite, the Indiana basketball thing."

It was his second year as a professor at Butler. Two years before, he had moved to Indiana from Minnesota.

"I was teaching a literary theory class. This is high theory, based on a critique of power, of culture, of media." The students were studying Debord, Marxist theory, using words like *detournement*. They unpacked difficult paragraphs that implied a knowledge of previous writers' difficult paragraphs, such as this one:

The alienation of the spectator to the profit of the contemplated object (which is the result of his own unconscious activity) is expressed in the following way: the more he contemplates the less he lives; the more he accepts recognizing himself in the dominant images of need, the less he understands his own existence and his own desires. The externality of the spectacle in relation to the active man appears in the fact that his own gestures are no longer his but those of another who represents them to him. This is why the spectator feels at home nowhere, because the spectacle is. . . .

Paragraphs that require some knowledge of Hegel, paragraphs that call into question even the possibility of a spectator sport that does not diminish the spectator or fan. Students of theory will immediately recognize the hypocrisy of the one-year-and-on-to-the-pros college basketball culture, the selling of even the high school athlete to the shoe and sports drink companies; they will see the belief that a team is tied to its fans by anything other than the profit motive as deluded or nostalgic.

The students in the class were from history, anthropology, classics, English. There were five graduate students in the class. High theory is one of the most difficult classes a humanities or social science student will take.

It's intellectual play with high stakes if taken seriously. The students in this class were the self-chosen intellectuals at Butler, the professor said, hardworking kids with IQs off the charts, near-perfect verbal SAT scores.

The thing about studying theory is that it gives rise to an ironic attitude (though irony itself can be appropriated), and "there is no irony in basketball," the professor explains. Indiana basketball is flat-out completely sincere, and its fans are sincere as though the whole intellectual history of the twentieth century never happened.

Even saying that you're sincere about something like basketball is difficult if you're a theorist because if you say anything sincerely you realize that you may have been manipulated into saying it by someone trying to make money from your sincerity.

So the night of the Syracuse game the students were in the Jordan Hall seminar room, and they were studying Althusser's essay "Ideology of the Ideological State Apparatus."

It's an influential essay from the late 1960s, an essay about how culture reproduces itself. "He's very vicious," the young professor said, "about how you can never get outside the culture of exploitation.

"As examples, he uses everyday things like going to the church, or school, or being in a family. These benign things are his definition of 'ideology' and they have a secondary purpose, which is to keep the status quo. And the purpose of the status quo is to keep us in a culture of exploitation."

The first hour the professor unpacked the dense language, so dense it's like a new language that must be learned in order to converse in it. Theory-speak, particle physics of the humanities. And these students, filled sometimes with so much irony that they don't even know when they're being serious and when they're not, they understand the language. They speak it. It's as though they've always spoken it. Lacan. Derrida. Foucault. They're cool. Outside of class, the students speak in film quotes, and they know they're speaking in film quotes and they know they've been manipulated to speak in film quotes and they manipulate the manipulation. They know the culture of the '80s as well as they know Milton. And they know Milton. And they know some Latin and they're studying Ancient Greek.

"I threw things at them last semester that I didn't think they'd be able to handle, but they did," the professor said.

What I'm trying to say here is that these kids are frickin smart and sometimes jaded in a pre-9/11 way, "the last group of kids that you would expect to be leveled" by something as earnest as Indiana basketball, according to the professor.

Even the language surrounding basketball in Indiana—all the books about the heroes and the statistics and the infamous last-minute shots, the whole narrative arc of the game and the postgame discussions in coffee shops around town squares by men and women on their way to work ("coffee shops," "town squares," "work"), are earnest. When you live in that mythology, you would not ever think for one second that you're being manipulated by capitalist forces—or rather, it's so obvious if you have grown up, say, in a small town and watched the factories breezing in and out, leaving behind a kind of after-the-party mess for you to clean up, so obvious as to go unstated. Your parents just hope they keep their jobs.

You would not bring theory to bear on basketball or think of it as an ideology. It is absolutely what it is and not what it appears to be, and you, the fan, are not a cultural construction. You are a human being and there's no use stopping to ask what that is. That's Indiana basketball.

"So we're talking about this critique of culture and it's the night of the Syracuse game, and being good Butler students, they all came to class."

"But there's a sort of rumbling about the game," he said, "which surprised me."

Still, the professor gave his lecture.

"And I realized that when we usually take a break, about an hour and a half into the evening class, that it should be around the last fifteen minutes of the game. At this point we'd stop and watch the end of it."

The young professor is blond and young and as cool as the students, or rather cooler. He is what they aspire to be. He has the cool glasses of an intellectual and the broad shoulders of a football player. He is both smart and funny. And he's kind.

"In Minnesota, I played individual sports," he says.

"And I didn't understand basketball really, what it meant here."

They could pick up the television in the classroom, through the computer, and project the image on a large screen.

At break they turned it on. Butler was winning, but it was a close game and within a few seconds Syracuse was ahead, 54–50. Syracuse was the number one seed and mid-major Butler was seeded number five. Everyone in the class knew what that could mean; they knew this was the point in the game where the more highly ranked team's experience and skill kick in, and they pull away. It's the moment every fan begins to feel part of the spectacle rather than simply an observer, when your own cheers and prayers and high-fives and most of all your complete attention to the action feels necessary to your team's win.

The kids were mostly Indiana kids, as was the team. They'd grown up going to high school basketball games on weekend nights. They'd grown up in towns where there were basketball hoops in all the driveways, where all the fathers took their turn at coaching.

"That night was when I understood the post-irony thing," the professor said, "and this deep connection between Indiana and basketball and Butler."

Number five seed Butler was playing Syracuse, the number one seed. But there's Ronald Nored, their friend; he's got the ball behind the three-point line and he shoots! Ronald is a 17 percent three-point shooter; his ball goes miraculously into the basket. The students in the classroom in Jordan Hall erupt. Their team! It's one point behind a number-one-ranked team. Right there on a screen that, just a few hours earlier had been showing excerpts of a Beckett play, a screen covering a whiteboard with the ghost images of calculations left by an afternoon math class, right there on that screen was the unfolding of a story where Butler was one point away from making it to the Elite Eight.

From that point until the end of the game there will be no analysis of the story, only the joy of the ride. Willie Veasley, the quiet one, is suddenly on fire. He tips in a missed shot! He sinks a three-pointer that at first (the suspense) circles the rim but finally brings the score to 58–54 Butler. And then, with 59 seconds left in the game, he lands a shot to bring the score to 60–54, a score where you can almost begin to believe you're going to win.

By the end of the game, everyone in the class was jumping up and down and screaming. Their team had made it to the Elite Eight! It was impossible, joyous.

They could hear students running out of their dormitories and fraternity or sorority houses, out of their apartments and onto the quad. They could hear the three hundred or so fans from the viewing party on the first floor of Jordan Hall. We're in the Elite Eight! We beat Syracuse!

"Baby-faced kids, really, screaming for other baby-faced kids," the professor said. Hoosier kids who understood both the language of academia and the language of their culture. They could both criticize it and live within it.

And at the end of the game, what do you do after an experience like that? With the rest of the campus celebrating outside the window of your classroom? "I mean, I'm not gonna lie," he said. "We were all excited. For the last few minutes of that game it's like we were ten years old.

"We had this earnest time where we regressed, and I'd given my lecture already, and it was time now for discussion. Now what do I do?" The professor laughed when he said this. He smiled and shrugged. This was the moment when he realized how much he loved these kids, his students, that he was happy to be here. He was happy for them.

But he had more material to cover. The students wanted to cover it. What more could you want in your life than to be teaching something you love, something that gives you joy to contemplate, ideas that are rich and complex, ideas that will lead to other ideas, ideas the contemplation of which will lead you back through the study of other rich and complex things: linguistics, philosophy, classics, economics. The cell. The universe. The fact that love exists.

They finished the class because, as the professor said, "These are Butler kids and this is what they do.

"So, I said, 'That was awesome and it was super fun and so what does it mean to read this essay and to experience this, how does college basketball, for instance, help to reproduce culture, how does it serve as an ideological apparatus that helps us reproduce the exploitation and power dynamics of capitalism?'

"I actually said that," he chuckled, "and I said it earnestly!

"Well, one of the kids said, 'It seems like there's a place here where there's a sanctioned violence.'"

Matt Howard, their friend, was always getting hit, always getting thrown down on the hardwood, up against the goal. That night he had been hit particularly hard. And every time he was hit, he got up and kept going. Once he was hit so hard he received a concussion and for a moment thought he was Larry Bird.

"'What about the difference between the cheerleaders and the male players,' one said, 'cheerleaders as spectacle in comparison to the male players as performers?'

"They were able to go back into critical mode while still being earnestly about school spirit," the professor said. "They were able to talk about symbolically reproduced power dynamics and to participate in the joy of the game and leave at the end of class, because of both, in a good mood."

Good game! Good class!

"Basketball," the professor said later, "is such a weird thing to me.

"I came from Minnesota, and it has a culture. Uptight Scandinavian, but a culture that goes back to Europe.

"For me, being an outsider, Indiana felt to me like a place without culture. I felt this kind of banality, even in nature. It's in the middle, landlocked; it felt claustrophobic.

"But I'm getting it. This made me get all of it. The concrete poured on the flatness, the *sublime* flatness, the stoic discipline in the repetition of the bounce, the movement up and down the court.

"For me, personally, the experience was one of finally being connected.

"We watched the other games with critics," he said. "People who aren't team athletes or usually enjoy spectacle athletics. And there was just no comparison between college basketball and the corporate professional version." We were all getting into it.

"And I could see how it used to be that way in high schools.

"And I understood how basketball can be this place of pure excitement and attention. Something pure.

"And there was a sense, during the tournament, that something great was about to happen, that something was about to change."

## ON BEING A FAN

*When spring came, even the false spring, there were no problems except where to be happiest.*
—ERNEST HEMINGWAY, *A MOVEABLE FEAST*

During the weeks of the tournament, the weather cooperated. You couldn't imagine a more beautiful place. It was a particularly seed-filled spring. Maple tree seeds were bountiful, and they came at your windshield as if you were driving through a snowstorm; the dry veined husks flew into your face and landed in your hair. As the spring went on, the seedlings grew in gutters, between sidewalk cracks. If two pieces of mulch were together on a driveway, a seed would sprout. It was as if they were trying to tell us something if we could only hear it.

The mailboxes in Jordan Hall are as old as the limestone building, small brass-faced boxes with combination locks that very seldom work. We all sit in our offices now and e-mail colleagues whose offices are two doors down from our own, and we e-mail our students and we have fewer meetings.

But when something happens in the university, we want to talk to someone, and we go to the mailroom and talk to Pam. She is the center of communication. Not a gossip: all the crazy bureaucratic low-stakes gossip takes place in the hallways. We go to Pam to remember life outside. She's the weather concierge, the sports concierge, the news concierge, the one who knows if a storm is coming and how fast, if the day will be too hot or too cold or just right. She notices us shiver as we come from in from the outside, and she speaks our thoughts out loud. "I'm not a fan of this heat," she'll say.

On nice days she keeps the window to the outside open and her office tunnels the breeze into the hallways.

Pam is the guard of the threshold. She makes it possible for us to move from one world to another with ease. If you want to talk about the last game, the area in front of the mailroom is where you go to talk about it.

She is, without doubt, the basketball team's biggest fan. A few years ago she started collecting clippings about the team and affixing them to the mailroom door, to the bulletin board by the window, to the walls inside the room, to the walls outside the room. If there was a center of public relations, where those of us who live in our books and classrooms became aware that something was growing, it was Pam. When the campus was filled with cameras and reporters, many of them would include her in their stories.

Right after 9/11 there were new announcements about the mail. The size, the heft, the way it might look if it was a bomb. Now you have to knock at the door to get inside the mailroom. Those signs are still there, someplace, but during basketball season they're buried underneath the *Chronicle* story about basketball and academics, underneath the *Times* and *Sports Illustrated* Xeroxes, and we're thankful for the break. The basketball clippings float on top of the warnings. We've internalized them by now and wouldn't see them even if they weren't covered by five or six layers of ecstatic clippings, drifting in from all over the country and landing in this rich layering around the mail-room window.

It started slowly. One article on the door. Then two, then four, then six-teen. You could come in first thing on Monday morning and the clippings would already be there, marked with Pam's thick marker, the important pas-sages highlighted as though they were pages in a textbook, the subject of which is Butler as seen through the lens of the team and compiled by Pam. *It was a wonderful year!* she'd have written. *They love our Shelvin Mack! Great moment! We love our Bulldogs!*

When you sit inside the mailroom with Pam, you realize it takes a certain type of person to do this job. Efficient, yet ebullient. Friendly so that people want to stop and talk, a kind of friendly that's like a gift you get to take with you. You always feel seen and noticed by Pam, and you feel cheered, but you never feel as though the thing you've come to do does not get done promptly or that the work itself is not important. The faces come rapidly to the window and each person has a piece of mail to move on, a stamp to buy, a question, and still you're her best friend and she talks to you as her hands efficiently move the mail. I can't stress enough how the faces appear and disappear in the rectangular window like the seeds coming at your windshield, like words coming up through a Magic Eight Ball. There's a refrain as the faces rise like fish out of the gray academic pond and into the window: No mail? one per-son says. Too much mail, says the next one. It toggles back and forth like that all day long.

Pam always wears a Butler blue shirt and khakis or jeans, and her hair is the same auburn as Gordon Hayward's mother, her cheeks the same shade of ruddy. Today is the day between the end of classes and the beginning of finals: "reading day."

A student, obviously stressed, comes by to get a stamp. Pam smiles and asks, "Have you read today?"

The student is taken aback. "It's reading day," Pam says. "So you should read something! Read a byline on a TV show. Read a menu!" The student gets her stamp and laughs and you can see the stress dissipating. That's Pam's gift.

Her love is the basketball team. Last Christmas she and her student staff took photos of the players, made them all little elves, and posted them on the door. That's how we got through that particular week of finals.

"Megan [her student assistant] and I noticed that Matt Howard played bet-ter when he wore a T-shirt under his jersey," she says. So they put a clipping of him not wearing a T-shirt outside the window with a sign that read "Matt! Put your shirt back on!"

"That's how I met Matt Howard," she says. The players always read the clippings, and Matt stopped by to say he didn't think it was true about the shirt. "He's very humble," Pam says. "He always takes the time to stop by now, to say hi."

"You know how the players get all wowed over?" She sees this in the hallways. She hears it. One day a girl was talking about how Matt Howard handed her a fork in the cafeteria. Pam sees everything. "Well Matt is so humble."

She laughs. "His father is a mailman, you know."

She remembers a time she was talking to Matt, about random things, and suddenly he took a banana out of his pocket. "You know the thing about bananas?" he asked with a grin.

"They take away cramps?" she asked.

"No," he laughed, "they contain the same drug as Prozac. They're a happy fruit."

And he took the banana and placed it, like a smile, in front of his mouth. His eyes smiled too. Then he put it upside down, and his eyes turned sad as a clown's.

"Mike Green used to love on me a lot," she says. "He'd leave will-call tickets." A mail lady's salary doesn't pay for basketball tickets, but everyone loves Pam so much they started leaving her tickets, even for the finals. She sat up high, and the floor looked like a postage stamp. She would know.

"God," she says, "I love Hinkle."

Where do you get all the articles? I ask her. She reads the paper and people send them to her. It's like a wiki of newspaper clippings, as complete as any media service could provide. There's a local broadcaster, Jake Query, quoted in the *Tampa Tribune*. "When I get back home," he says, "I'm going to get the newspaper headline that said Butler is going to the Final Four, get it laminated, take it to my grandfather's grave, dust off his stone and lay it on top." *It was a wonderful year!* Pam adds.

Right next to the earnest "Are you in the know about return addressing?" U.S. Postal Service poster is a tongue-in-cheek article from the *Wall Street Journal*. "Just jump on the Butler bandwagon. Don't be embarrassed—we're all going to be shameless about this one. A couple of weeks back, most of us barely knew who they were. If someone asked you where Butler University was, you'd have said 'Err . . . In Butler?'

"Butler doesn't have a single starter taller than 5'2," they travel to away games on mules; and until last year, they played all of their home games by candlelight on a dirt floor."

*But we're all Bulldogs now!* Pam writes.

So how did this start? I ask her. "It's Mike Green that I fell in love with, and Pete Campbell and A.J. [Graves].

"A.J. still comes by, and he always talks to me and stops to read the clippings."

Every year after graduation she takes down clippings and puts them in a folder marked with the year. She can't take them down too early because the boys will notice.

When she started pulling down the collection this year, she felt someone looking at her and turned around. "It was Ronald Nored," she says. "And I was taking down the article about his grandma."

She let the article stay.

She's showing me her collection. "There's Coach," she says, pointing to a photo. "With Willie [Veasley]." Eventually the collection makes it to the Rare Books Room in Irwin Library.

The boys would stop by to say hello on their way to class. Willie, for instance, is notoriously shy, and Pam is good for shy people. She pulls you inside out, like extroverts sometimes do.

I think she became a bit of a mother to the boys. "I love those boys," she says. She mentions boys who don't get as much playing time. Emerson Kampen and Garrett Butcher. She loves them all.

And Coach Brad Stevens. "It's like he's a horse whisperer, but he's a basketball whisperer.

"You just have to trust him. I don't agree with him all the time, but you have to trust him."

She puts articles about the other sports teams up as well, but they don't get as much press. And there's something about the way the basketball boys stay together. They come to classes after early morning workouts. They laugh and talk. "They're like a flock of birds sometimes," she says. Or they're lonely.

They would tell her they were on their way to a test and would stop by on their way out of Jordan Hall to report on it. "Drew Streicher was so smart," she said "it didn't matter what he did. He was just brilliant."

One day Ryan Waggoner told her that it was Shelvin Mack's birthday and when she saw him in the hallway later in the day she sang "You say it's your birthday" to him. And Shelvin laughed and giggled because, Pam said in a very motherly teasing way, "you know that's mostly what he does."

She loves small college basketball.

"Dear Lord," she says, "I love Gonzaga."

"Except when they play us," she says.

"Gonzaga and Butler, they're better than any NBA game ever. I don't care about the NBA," she says. "I'd rather watch baseball than the NBA, and baseball is boring."

There's nothing better, she says, than college ball when it's played right. "My husband and I," she says, "it's like date night when we get tickets. The students are there, and all the staff and faculty. Shelvin Mack's family has those tiny bleacher seats and Shelvin's family is big. This is not gonna work, they kept saying.

But they were all stuffed in together with the rest of the crowd. Pam and her husband sat behind them, high-fiving and cheering.

So how was the mailroom different during the tournament?

"It was," Pam said, "the most insane thing I ever saw in my life.

"This is something that should be told," she says. After the Syracuse game, she and her student assistants were mailing T-shirts all over the world. "New York," she says. "South Carolina, Alaska, Texas, Florida. Overseas.

"People were mailing them by the ones and twelves and by the hundreds." People would go to the bookstore or to the Sigma Chi house, where an alum was selling shirts, and bring their bounty to the mailroom. Little kids, parents, grandparents, she said. And all the shirts had to be there before the next game. People could have ordered them online, but they wanted them to come to Butler, to be part of the whole festival.

When she's not in the mailroom, Pam is a master gardener. A week ago there was a sale on heirloom native plants at the Indianapolis Museum of Art, and she and a friend from Butler purchased a carful of perennials and vegetables.

And the faces still keep coming at her window. Faces so beautiful it almost breaks your heart, and she sees every one of them.

"We can never have another year like this year," she says. "It was incredible," she says. The whole ride.

"It's pretty bad that you only get to bloom for one season." Seriously. She says that.

---

. . . as I had come to find myself relying on the Giants as a life-giving, an exalting force, I found myself unable to relax in the company of "unbelievers," in the company of those who did not take their football earnestly or who thought my team something less than the One God. At those times, in those alien places, I felt like a holy man attempting to genuflect amidst a gang of drunken, babbling, mocking heretics.

—FRED EXLEY, *A FAN'S NOTES*

## HOW SURREAL WAS IT?

CNN'S Anderson Cooper called President Fong's office to let him know they were sending a team of reporters to find out if the players were really going to class.

Go ahead! Bobby said. We have nothing to hide.

An NCAA official joked about Avery Jukes and Gordon Hayward's math and science courses. Avery said there was so much mention of that it was like "the Beakers will be taking on the Bunsen Burners."

And when we saw Gordon and Avery leaving math class on Friday morning, we felt like applauding.

Blue the Bulldog hosted a party at the Good Dog Hotel and Spa, where they serve high-class dog-tinis, while our president and his wife, who have always refused to act presidential, continued to walk their rescue dogs. In the topsy-turvy world of the tournament the very democratic nature of their non-aristocratic ways seemed suddenly beautifully presidential. It felt mythically American, like John and Abigail Adams in the early White House, when it was all ordinary and dusty and being built. And in that sense of myth it was surreal.

And the night we beat Kansas State, advancing improbably to the Final Four, President Fong came out of the viewing party in Jordan Hall 141, and there were hundreds if not a thousand students on the mall. Some football players lifted him up on their shoulders and there was our president crowd-surfing the mosh pit of students. He trusted them! "Suzanne and I made our way over to Hampton," he said later. "We had come out of the building to what was a deafening roar. It was completely unexpected, and we were completely bowled over by the energy."

But how surreal is that to see your top administrator being carried hand to hand across a crowd?

It was the televised thing, the fact that those big events generally hit us in the Midwest more slowly, moved across the country in waves, and this was, except for the microscopically brief satellite delays, instantaneous.

How surreal is that?

And the governor kept having the team and the president and old players like Bobby Plump over to his house for barbecues.

Is that surreal?

The Chinese consul went to one of those barbecues at the governor's house, and he left early so he could stop by the Butler bookstore before it closed. He wanted to buy a T-shirt.

## ANOTHER VOICE: AN ALUM

What was it like? I was physically ill from nervousness the entire two weeks and all the symptoms were gone the Tuesday after the Duke game. I wanted them to win more than anything I've ever wanted in my life. But I think I would have been relieved either way.

It was crazy living downtown. For the Final Four semifinals it was packed everywhere. You couldn't even walk on the sidewalk. And after Butler won, everyone was yelling and running through the streets.

The funniest thing was when I went to work and everyone suddenly had Butler shirts on.

I wonder how many people have had more success with job interviews or getting into graduate school.

When did I cry? I cried when they went to the Final Four, after they beat Kansas State.

I cried after the championship game. I was so sad, but then walking home from Lucas Oil I got over it. After I saw how close that last shot had been on ESPN, I flipped out.

Day to day every once in a while it hits me.

## ON TEACHING

Chemistry professor Dr. Robert Pribush has taught at Butler for thirty-seven years, his own one and only life woven tightly into the fabric of the place.

Ten years ago he lost his seventeen-year-old son in a car accident, and he began that period of intense grief, numbness, and bargaining Joan Didion describes so well in her memoir *The Year of Magical Thinking*.

I mention this because I want to explore how an individual life is tied to a place, and how following the thread of an individual's life, of any life, will lead you back into the story of the community.

President Bobby Fong speaking at alumni brunch under portrait of Tony Hinkle. *Photograph by Brent Smith*

"It was an extended celebration, and the hours were long. By the end, most of us were just running on adrenaline."
— BOBBY FONG

Butler "Player of the Decade" A.J. Graves with Coach Brad Stevens and Athletic Director Barry Collier. *Photograph by Brent Smith*

"There was something in Tony Hinkle that was articulated again by Coach Barry Collier and is there in Stevens."
— BUTLER FACULTY MEMBER

Future Bulldogs at the Butler Campus Fair.
*Photograph by Brent Smith*

"Even though they were so young,
they knew all the players' names."
—BUTLER TOUR GUIDE

(Tarkington Street Fair) Ronald Nored's grandmother, Delores Kennedy-Williams.
*Photograph by Brent Smith*

When Pam started pulling down the collection this year, she felt
someone looking at her and turned around. "It was Ronald Nored," she says.
"And I was taking down the article about his grandma." She let it stay.

Butler bookstore pilgrims. *Photograph by Brent Smith*

"There were a ton of alumni walking around campus, telling you how it used to be."
—STUDENT

Final Four shootaround. *Photograph by Brent Smith*

"There was really no reason to root against them. They were everyone's Bulldogs!"
—A BUTLER FAN

Blue the bulldog and fans, and (*inset*) the plush ones waiting for a home.
*Photographs by Brent Smith*

"We have fourth graders writing notes. One of them wrote that she was jumping up and down on the couch during the games." —BUTLER STUDENT AND TOUR GUIDE

Superstar Blue. *Photograph by Brent Smith*

Blue was suddenly a star. Wherever he went, there were cameras snapping.

Coach Brad Stevens.
*Photograph by Brent Smith*

"To what extent does he know about
the calm that radiates from him?
Is he conscious of the way his
personality is producing
excellence all around him?"
—BUTLER FACULTY MEMBER

Junior Matt Howard signs autographs. *Photograph by Brent Smith*

"I heard President Bush the first say in a speech one time that when he thinks
of Indiana, he thinks of trees, kids, and basketball." —FATHER OF PLAYER

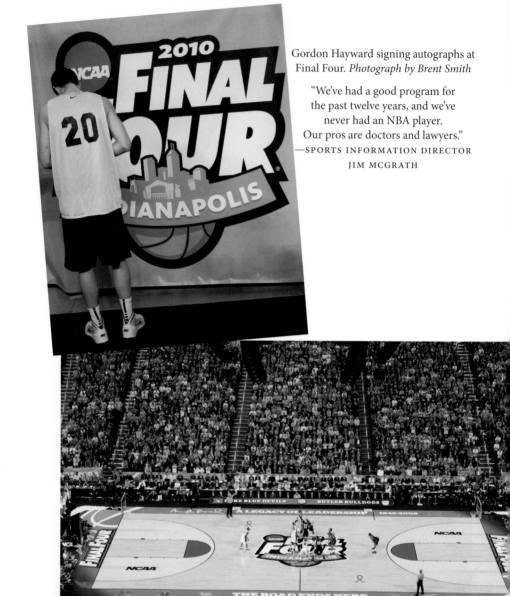

Gordon Hayward signing autographs at Final Four. *Photograph by Brent Smith*

"We've had a good program for the past twelve years, and we've never had an NBA player. Our pros are doctors and lawyers."
—SPORTS INFORMATION DIRECTOR JIM MCGRATH

The game begins. *Photograph by Brent Smith*

"I took a good friend of mine. He described it best: 'Epic.'" —BUTLER STUDENT

Pregame huddle.
*Photograph by Brent Smith*

"It was like, wow, these are the guys we go to school with every day, and live with, and eat breakfast with."
—BUTLER STUDENT

Butler students at championship game. *Photograph by Brent Smith*

"You are on fire and we are on fire with you!" —BUTLER STUDENT

Junior Shawn Vanzant.
*Photograph by Brent Smith*

Vanzant, who ties the
championship game at 16.
All the players are in this game to win.

Sophomore Gordon Hayward.
*Photograph by Brent Smith*

"Like I told people, it was all
surreal. As a sophomore, I lived
in ResCo along with Gordon and
Ron and all the guys. I have a
class with Ron now. I was watching my friends out there."
—STUDENT

Coach Brad Stevens.
*Photograph by Brent Smith*

"It's like he's a horse whisperer,
but he's a basketball whisperer.
You just have to trust him."
—PAM HOPKINS, MAIL PROCESSOR

Junior Zach Hahn.
*Photograph by Brent Smith*

Zach Hahn comes off the
bench and scores three points!
Like he's saying, *I don't need
to dribble. I come off the bench
and I'm ready. Put me in!*

Sophomore Ronald Nored.
*Photograph by Brent Smith*

"The kids who'd been working
with Ronald gave me a
blue and white scarf that they'd
brought for Blue the dog."
—JUDITH LYSAKER, COLLEGE
OF EDUCATION PROFESSOR

The road ends here. *Photograph by Brent Smith*

"I stood there, looking down at this group of boys that had brought not just a stadium
but the whole nation to its feet. And I couldn't contain my pride and happiness. It's a
feeling that has lasted far longer than the disappointment of not raising that trophy."
—BUTLER ALUM

Dawg Pound.
*Photograph by Brent Smith*

"So I just started running,
and so did everyone else.
It was a big field of energy!"
—BUTLER STUDENT AND FAN

Sophomore Shelvin Mack.
*Photograph by Brent Smith*

It was Mack who made
seven three-pointers
in the first round against
UTEP. And in this game
it's Mack's three-point shot
at 14:06 that brings
the team's spirit back.

Junior Matt Howard.
*Photograph by Brent Smith*

As a center, his job is to get hit
and to keep on going.

Senior Avery Jukes (24) with (*from left*) Assistant Coach Micah Shrewsberry,
Shawn Vanzant, Grant Leiendecker, Coach Brad Stevens, and Matt Howard.
*Photograph by Brent Smith*

"I had women tell me they literally had tears in their eyes
during the game. I think people feel a deep, intense connection to the team."
—DEB SMITH, MOTHER OF FRESHMAN PLAYER ANDREW SMITH

Senior Willie Veasley. *Photograph by Brent Smith*

"Ask Coach Veasley! Coach Veasley
was at the game!"
—STUDENT,
BRAD STEVENS BASKETBALL CAMP

Hinkle Field house interior. *Photograph by Brent Smith*

"It's getting hard to get people out of Hinkle. They'll just stand in front of the basketball
picture and stare at it, or stand on the court in Hinkle and look up and spin in circles."
—BUTLER STUDENT AND TOUR GUIDE

Final Four pep rally. *Photograph by Brent Smith*

"There was a madness that consumed the campus." —BUTLER STUDENT

Student athletes surrounded by trophies at 2010 commencement:
Willie Veasley, Avery Jukes, Nick Rodgers, and Alex Anglin. *Photograph by John Fetcho*

"He'll keep recruiting this type of player." —BUTLER ALUM

Gordon Hayward cutting the net after West Coast Regional Championship game. *Photograph by John Fetcho*

The joy on Hayward's face is unlike anything, just the pure smile as he goes onto the court. He smiles with his eyes.

Celebrate! *Photograph by John Fetcho*

You're only young once and it's spring on an idyllic midwestern college campus and it feels suddenly like all the world's attention has descended on you.

West Regional champs! *Photograph by John Fetcho*

We could easily have worshipped those boys on the team and their blue-eyed coach. We didn't, because we knew them well before the gods descended.

West Regional celebration. *Photograph by John Fetcho*

Such height when they jump! Such control of their bodies in the air!

Every August a new class of eighteen-year-old kids arrives on a university campus and every year you tell yourself you won't fall in love again, but you do. Over and over again the students pass through your classes. You recognize types as the years go on. You watch the parade of names, the popularity of certain names and even letters—the students from the decade when every student's name began with J (the Jennifers and Joshuas and Jasons) and the year the Dylans and Ethans first appeared. You may notice the popularity of a certain type of glasses (they narrow then widen then disappear entirely) or of shoes, the rise and fall of the waist on jeans. After thirty-seven years you can compress it and see it as time-lapse photography; you can visualize the styles of hair like flowers opening and closing while the faces stay so similar, so young. But by October of every year you've begun to see each one as an individual and you get pulled into their stories. You'll forget the names of some in a semester or so, but you'll always recognize the faces and, depending on what you teach, you'll remember certain things about them and what they accomplished.

But when you lose your own child at seventeen, Bob explains to me, you wonder how you can continue teaching young people. Knowing that your own child will never be that age. The constant reminder of that, the grieving, the anger.

Teachers continue to be present in the classroom, to collect their paychecks and put in their time while pulling back, giving less, with much less provocation. In the essay "Where Have All the Fifty-Five-Year-Olds Gone?," in her book *Letters from the Country,* the writer Carol Bly described how people in their fifties seem to disappear from institutions they once were so involved in because they realize they've given so much to something that will never give back and in so doing have neglected their own souls. And so they pull away. Or they spread poison. (We tried that fifteen years ago and it failed then and will fail again, etc.)

Looking for something that would allow him to continue, Dr. Pribush began by talking to the Lutheran minister who had conducted the funeral service for his son, a man who seemed "to grasp the situation," an unthinkable one, "so well."

The journey itself is a private one, and so I will leave it to Bob to tell. I will only say that the journey was spiritual, and it led him to the point where he now carefully weighs things he will spend (and it is an economy, that word that has lost its meaning) his time on. "I haven't changed in all these years," he says. "I've just become more aware that my calling is teaching but that I'm not here to teach chemistry as much as I'm here to help mold lives."

Either you become angry because none of these boys is your son or you realize that each one of the students with whom you come in contact is in some way, for better or worse, your son or daughter.

When each basketball player was asked to bring one teacher with him to the governor's mansion for an end-of-semester barbecue celebrating the team's achievement, forward Avery Jukes invited Dr. Pribush. And at a post-season benefit at the NCAA headquarters in downtown Indianapolis Avery's own proud parents were there. And there was Bob with his camera, taking everything in, taking hundreds of photos, the lens of his camera on Avery, the latest incarnation of his own lost son.

"I've told Avery 'I follow your games because you have an enormously good heart.' And I've learned from him how to relax and slow down." Professor and player have molded each other.

The story, or the part of it I'm going to tell, begins in Uganda in 1961 when Joseph Koni, leader of the Lord's Resistance Army was born. From all accounts Koni was (and is—he's still reportedly alive) one of those charismatic but psychotic people who, for whatever reason, gains power but has a delusional system he's able to force on those who are weaker. He claimed he was a Christ figure. Koni's army abducted an estimated 30,000 children from their homes in Uganda and displaced another 1.6 million. In the beginning he made the children stand in cross-shaped groups, and he would paint the shape of a cross on their chests and tell the children it would stop the enemy's bullets. The plight of these children gave rise to the Invisible Children, an organization dedicated to supporting and giving voice to those abducted Ugandan children.

"The children were brainwashed, drugged, given alcohol, and in some cases forced to kill their own parents," Dr. Pribush explains.

A Butler student had written papers on Uganda for her global and historical studies course, and she was so moved by her studies that she brought the Invisible Children group to campus to speak. "That was the beginning of a growing awareness on the Butler campus of problems in Uganda," he says.

In 1998 an Indianapolis travel agency had formed a nonprofit group called Global Ambassadors for Children (GAC). Butler biology major Michael Hole, recounted Bob, "had been in a class of mine along with fellow biology major Stephanie Steele," and during Michael's junior year at Butler, he asked his professor to serve as adviser for a Butler chapter of Global Ambassadors for Children.

The organization was planning a trip to Uganda and invited Bob to go with them as adviser. "When Michael first mentioned Uganda," Bob said, he flipped: "All I could think of was Idi Amin."

But he went to a State Department website and found that Uganda was, at the time, stable. "So five of us from Butler went along with two students from the University of Alabama on a GAC trip. We went to Uganda for seventeen days, spending most of our time in Kampala."

The first day they were there, he explains, the World Food Organization delivered 110 pounds of grain and cooking oil, and the group from Butler distributed it. They went out with social workers and would visit half a dozen homes in a few hours. "The thing that impressed you most," Dr. Pribush explained, "was that people were so loving and didn't hesitate to invite you into their homes, feed you plantains. Kids would yell out, come up and give you hugs. It was incredible. Powerful.

"You say to yourself, Here are the poorest people on earth, and they may be the happiest. You come back here and people are bitching and moaning about everything. All the students who went on that trip came back motivated to help others.

"In the next year Michael Hole raised $40,000, and when we went back, we built a school."

In 2007 "Avery [Jukes] was in my chemistry class. At the time he was in the five-year engineering program. I had talked to the class about my experience in Uganda, and right after class that day Avery came to my office. He said he wanted to go. I told him he'd have to talk to his coach. Brad said yes, which I thought was phenomenal.

"What Avery experienced there—" Here Bob can't quite find the words. "We were staying in a hotel, and there were young boys who slept there at night."

Avery wanted to know why, and he was told by the hotel management that they were boys hiding from the Koni troop abductions.

"We got back from Uganda," Bob says, and one day "Avery looked in my door and said 'I'm gonna start a foundation.'

"And within a month he'd started a foundation and raised enough money to send five kids to school for a year."

"Before Avery went to Uganda," his mother says to me, "it was all about Avery. And when he came back, I could tell in his voice that he was a different person."

It's after the tournament and we are at the NCAA headquarters in down-town Indianapolis, where most of the team has gathered to sign autographs and raise funds for what is now known as the Avery Jukes Foundation. The headquarters is located next to the Indiana State Museum, at the site of an old grain elevator and mill.

Coach Brad Stevens steps to the microphone. "Avery came into my office the January of his junior year," Brad Stevens says. "I thought he was coming in to talk to me about playing more.

"But what he said was 'Do you care if I go on a mission trip this summer?'"

"The most important thing I did in my life was go on a mission trip. I came back not a changed man but an affected man," says the coach.

"So I told Avery he should go."

In his speech, Stevens says he remembers taking the team to Italy. "We went to the Colosseum. I said they didn't build the Colosseum to be torn down a few years later. They built it to last for eternity."

"I'm proud of Avery because he's continued to follow through," and he quotes from the book he quoted from before the championship game, the 1906 *As a Man Thinketh:* "Men attract not that which they want, but that which they are."

He turns his thoughts back to Uganda. "By nightfall today, 10,000 children will die of hunger. It's like a Haiti every day."

I'm no theologian, but there is religion in its best form and in its worst, the demonic and the divine, as Paul Tillich might say, woven throughout this story.

What comes out of it, you hope, is not an ideology but an ethos.

Can an ethos spread? "It can," Bob says. "And it does."

It can spread like a rumor can spread, like a virus. There was something in Tony Hinkle, he explains, that went dormant but was articulated again by Coach Barry Collier and is there in Stevens. "Bobby [Fong] has brought a global sense to the campus. He's helped different groups get a sense of equality. And then Brad said to his team, 'The expectations for you are now higher, and you have to accept that.'"

"Brad seems sort of special," Bob says. "What I want to say is that the thing with Avery and with Brad, it's not an illusion. This is real."

## ON HISTORY

Ronald Nored, College of Education professor Judy Lysaker explains, volunteers with at-risk four-year-olds in the Indianapolis Public Schools. "We know Mr. Nored," they said to her when she visited the classroom. "The kids who'd been working with Ronald gave me a blue and white scarf that they'd brought for Blue the dog."

"Ronald had talked to those kids about wanting to be a teacher."

I'm talking to the Judys: Lysaker and Cebula. Judy Lysaker is a reading specialist and professor. Judith Cebula is the former religion editor of the *Indianapolis Star* and administrator of the Center for Faith and Vocation on the Butler campus.

What makes all of this such a big deal, Cebula explains, is that we won but we can also do *this*. The service.

But Cinderella has only one season. The question is what continues after the ball. "When Cinderella moves into the castle, she brings her identity with her. So the question is, what will she take with her. Is she still going to feed the chickens? Does she stay nice and kind, the good sister, or does she get corrupted by wealth and power? And how do you keep that from happening?"

Judith, by virtue of her position and temperament, is a person who raises questions, who invites conversation. Why did we all love Tony Hinkle so much? He had a commitment to the university and the university had a commitment to him. What do we retain from him, perhaps unconsciously? Did Barry Collier pick up on that, and how? Was it transmitted directly or is it woven into the fabric of the institution in some invisible way?

And how does that tie into the community?

"Conseco and Lucas Oil are clearly an homage to the fieldhouse," Cebula says. "But Conseco doesn't feel like Hinkle. It's like Buca di Beppo. When you first go in there, it feels like one of those small cafes in Italy. But soon you realize it's a franchise of the real thing. A fake, a fraud."

There's still something charming about Hinkle. "So how do we hold on to that? How do we keep it real? Are the Hinkle upgrades going to make it more like Conseco or preserve what's real? Are we going to have some conversations about that?"

What can continue is the text itself, she explains. The Way.

It's interesting, Cebula says, that Brad Stevens is a Methodist. "If I weren't

Catholic, I'd be a Methodist," she says. The focus on finding the truth, the epistemology, in Methodism is through the experience, the text, and the tradition. When one loses its meaning for you, say the text, then you rely on your experience of God. If you lose the direct experience, you turn to the text. When you lose both, you rely for a while on the tradition.

Our connection to the tradition or history is what we lost for a while. "We're divorced from our own history. It's like your family did this amazing thing, and we never talk about."

The university was founded by an abolitionist. From the beginning, there were important women faculty members. Butler's first African American student, Gertrude Amelia Mahorney, graduated in the class of 1887.

"The tournament came and it's like a front went through," said Judy. It was as though a fog we'd been laboring under was somehow lifted and some true experience was revealed, revealing in turn the text and the tradition, revivifying all of it.

"It's tough," she said. "You have to live in a way that is visible in the world but without calling attention to itself. You don't brand it if one of your core values is humility. You let it unfold."

In Admissions, say, how do you recruit the type of student-athlete that you're looking for? You invite them and they become that type of person because of the culture, she says. You have to be clear about what that culture is.

"When you're invited to the monastery, you know what you're invited to."


## HINKLE FIELDHOUSE

Several years ago I was walking through an antique store in Indianapolis and I ran across two Butler yearbooks from 1928 and 1929. They're sitting on my desk in front of me as I write. Now and then I'll take them into a class and show the students. I was attracted to them because they're beautiful books. I couldn't even begin to tell you how they were made. They're both embossed leather, hand-stitched. The '29 version has the face of a bulldog, raised so that it's three-dimensional, on the cover; one half of its face is black with a black eye and the other half silver with a silver eye. The bulldog's eyes and nostrils are indentations in the leather, and its jowls are the highest point. It has five perfect white leather teeth. The background is made to look like bark, so the face is growing out of a tree.

There are color plates of the campus hand-glued (you can tell by the slightest tilt), like postcards, onto thick creamy pages with borders like William Morris wallpapers.

After the postcards there are two beautiful and leisurely handmade paper pages devoted entirely to a line drawing of Jordan Hall ("a beautiful and preposterous dream," said those who were against moving the campus from Irvington to the east side of Indianapolis) and to this note:

*Dear Friends:*
*You noticed the bull on the front page of this book, didn't you?*
*Well, the book itself might be considered a china shop.*

I love trying to imagine the students who wrote this. There are beautiful pages of thick onionskin paper with single phrases on them. Phrases like AT LAST! Most of the pages have embossed green vines drawn around them, letters hidden in the same green ink among the leaves, like a subliminal message. *Still drifting?* it reads at the top of a page. *Yes, still drifting* is written at the bottom.

The book is divided into sections, its division pages inspirational portraits of Mark Twain ("America's Mystic") and William Makepeace Thackeray and Stephen Foster. All the way through the book there are parodies. Parodies of advertisements. (Adbusters, anyone?) Parodies of celebrity. (The campus "big shot" whose name the reporter can't get right; who eats a plate of cherries with the reporter and accidentally puts his hand into his mouth instead of the spoon.)

While all the editors are men, the staff is more than 50 percent women, as is the membership of the Math Club and the Zoology Club. Butler was founded in 1855 by an abolitionist, Ovid Butler. It was the first college west of the Alleghenies to endow a professorial chair specifically for a woman. In the Midwest, only Oberlin and Butler admitted women to "regular" classes. We have forgotten most of those things over the years.

Butler Fieldhouse, now Hinkle, the setting we all know from *Hoosiers,* was built in 1928. It was, as sportswriter Howard Caldwell wrote in his 1991 book *Tony Hinkle: Coach for All Seasons,* "like no other basketball facility in the nation save Madison Square Garden."

In 1928 basketball was a much slower game. The center jump was still required after every point, and a big defensive player could stand under the basket as long as he wanted and just bat away the balls.

Smack dab in the center of the book, after Twain and before Thackeray, there's a line drawing of Paul "Tony" Hinkle. It's not a particularly good likeness, but like all good caricatures it gets certain things right and is unmistakable. Wavy hair parted in the middle, the crooked bow tie. The portrait of Hinkle follows a portrait of other male administrators. *The Boys Who Run Things* is written on the next page.

"But, all feelings of school patriotism aside," the editor writes, "Butler's athletic future really does, at present, look remarkably bright."

*Yes, still drifting.* I suspect there's a bit of the English major's irony in that Boys Who Run Things heading or even that one of the girls who made up the majority of the staff wrote the line.

Blue II is widely thought to be our second bulldog mascot. I'm here to tell you there was a bulldog mascot in 1929. And the day-care center we've been talking about for years? Butler's Department of Education ran a day nursery on North New Jersey called the Claire Ann Shover Nursery School. There are pictures in this yearbook. It was open every day of the week from 9:30 to 4:30.

In 1929 Butler "played the very best teams in the country and defeated all of them, usually winning by large scores." North Carolina, Pittsburgh, Indiana, Purdue, Missouri. Every team was beaten. "Butler had as good a claim as any other school this year to the national title," the yearbook writer writes.

And so there are those two banners hanging in Hinkle, claiming the national title for Butler in 1924 and 1929. The NCAA single-elimination tournament began in 1939, but before that, teams came to Indianapolis simply to play in Hinkle Fieldhouse itself and national titles were more loosely defined. In 1962, Butler won its first NCAA tourney under Hinkle. Hinkle retired as coach in 1970, and for a while basketball became less of a priority for the university. The Indiana high school basketball finals were played in the fieldhouse, and Butler basketball was important to the Indianapolis community, but it wasn't until the 1980s that the university began, largely under President Geoffrey Bannister, to put resources and attention back into the basketball program. It was a conscious decision by Bannister, a native of New Zealand, to rebuild a program he recognized was important to the history and culture of the campus and community. In 1985 we won the NIT. In 1987 Darrin Fitzgerald shot 153 three-point shots, an NCAA record. And after that, the team consistently landed in the tournament and then began landing in the Sweet 16.

Hinkle coached forty-one seasons at Butler and was associated with the university until his death in 1992. For years he lived on the corner of Hampton and Sunset, and he was often seen pulling weeds around the fieldhouse. There's a direct line, a handshake, between Hinkle and the later coaches including Collier, Matta, Lickliter, the current assistant coaches, and Brad Stevens.

To see the origins of Hinkle Fieldhouse, you go back to the yearbook of 1928. The 1928 yearbook is perhaps even more visually stunning. The same embossed leather but this time with a complex cover design of three triangles, the top one a basketball-colored (though not at that time) rendering of Jordan Hall. The angles of the cover are continued in the frontispiece design, and the yearbook includes lithographs by a Butler student who would become a well-known artist, Jane Messick, in the German *sachplakat* or "fact poster" design. They're reminiscent of the South Shore Line posters or posters for the London Underground in the 1920s. They were, in other words, very cool and very contemporary at the time. They still are.

In order to build a place to play basketball that wasn't a barn, the architect needed the new technology of the arched steel clear-span truss system. This way there were no poles in the way of viewers. In addition, the walls needed to be brick for fireproofing.

And so the fieldhouse, a six-story building on three acres, cost close to one million dollars to build. It was one of the first buildings to go up on the new Butler campus when the college moved from Irvington. From its completion in 1928 until the 1950s it was the largest basketball arena in the country. The funding for its construction came from a corporation of forty-one Indiana donors and was built with the understanding that Butler would always allow the Indiana High School Athletic Association tournament to be played there.

In the beginning, the fieldhouse wasn't named after Tony Hinkle, but it was Hinkle who advocated for it. And it was Hinkle who in many ways made the particular form of basketball we play today. Before Hinkle, basketballs were the brown leather of footballs. It was Hinkle who invented the orange ball so that it could be seen by players and fans. He was on the national collegiate rules committee that helped change the rules that had originally favored the tall guy, in part because it was good for his style of game. "A lot of smaller players went to Butler," Caldwell writes, "because they were told by larger schools that they were too small to play."

This is of course still true.

And it was Hinkle who created what was at the time called the Hinkle System: the constant movement of the ball between pairs of players and what we refer to now as picks and screens. "Everybody has a place to go and the ball keeps moving" is the way he described it.

"He was tough, but he wasn't a shouter or one who would rake you over the coals all the time," a 1926 graduate said. "He would explain your faults and tell you how to correct them instead of yelling. He was a gentle sort of coach."

In 1929 one of his players said: "He'd get after you if he didn't think your feet were moving fast enough. I've never seen a fellow create quick feet, but he could do it."

Because of the fieldhouse, coaches in the 1920s would bring their teams to Indianapolis, on their way to other games, just to play Butler. "It was," Caldwell wrote, "a first rate recruiting tool."

It's hard to conceive of this, but in 1928, basketball was only thirty-seven years old. It was a game invented as a lark, a way to train football players during the severe New England winters.

The fieldhouse and the Butler program weren't without controversy. In the 1930s the North Central Association briefly took away Butler's accreditation, citing the expenditure of close to a million dollars for a sports facility. "A million dollar athletic facility with nearly half again as much invested in equipment," critics called it. For a while the new campus was called "a Fieldhouse in search of a university."

Butler had a basketball team in 1892–93. The first Indiana high school tournament was played in 1911. That's how far back, and how entwined with its history, the tradition of basketball and Butler go. Seventeen thousand people gathered to celebrate Tony Hinkle's last game. After his first win, classes were dismissed.

Over the years, the fieldhouse has hosted seven American presidents, including Herbert Hoover, Bill Clinton, and Barack Obama. It was commandeered as a barracks for soldiers and sailors during World War II. Jesse Owens ran 60 yards in 6.1 seconds in 1939 in Hinkle, running into hay bales that were set up so he wouldn't crash into the stands.

Why is it always about the ending, I wonder? The landing of the gymnast or the ballerina. The last page of a book. The last shot of a game. Of course it's either death or a new beginning, but does everything come down to the good death?

Before this tournament, there were two big moments in Indiana basketball history. The first was in 1954 when Milan upset Muncie Central. The second was in 1955 when Oscar Robertson led Crispus Attucks to the state title. The tournament is now number three.

One of the reasons this tournament felt so surreal was that we didn't understand where it had come from. The tradition was invisible, but it was there. It was always there.

## LIGHTNESS OF BEING

Judith Cebula is interested in how the values of the Butler Way, as expressed in our history by Tony Hinkle and reformulated by athletic director Barry Collier, might become a basis for a campus conversation. Because, she says, there was really something there, something that rose up during the games. "With all the media participation," she explains, "the bullshit detector would have been on, and they saw something here."

The Butler Way was first articulated by Tony Hinkle as a style of playing that "demands commitment, denies selfishness, accepts reality yet seeks constant improvement while promoting the good of the team above self." Barry Collier, first as coach and later as athletic director, reformulated the philosophy, and the core values of the approach hang in the Butler locker room: humility (know who we are, strengths and weaknesses); passion (do not be lukewarm, commit to excellence); unity (do not divide our house, team first); servanthood (make teammates better, lead by giving); and thankfulness (learn from every circumstance).

The phrase "the Butler Way" came up often during the tournament as a way of describing Butler's particular style of ball and the values of the coach and players. It is always tempting in sports to see a win as the validation of a political system or set of values. When Butler University made it into the finals of the NCAA basketball tournament, we wanted to believe that in this case it was true. We played the game the right way. We lived these values, and both the coach and players were evidence of that. The boys were humble, on and off the court. They were passionate about the game but also about schoolwork and service. They were team players, not hot-shots. "These are really good guys" is the consensus of any student you talk to. Butler is a small school. If they weren't good guys, we would know.

And Coach Stevens? His story is legendary in the community. A DePauw University graduate, he had a good full-time job at Eli Lilly, the pharmaceutical company. But his passion was basketball, and so he quit his job and became a full-time volunteer in the basketball program at Butler. So far in this story we have humility, passion, and servanthood.

While a volunteer, he worked with the team, and when Todd Lickliter left the head coaching position for the University of Iowa, Brad Stevens was named head coach. He led the Bulldogs to the finals, leading to speculation that he would be recruited by a larger school with a much larger budget than Butler's. But he stayed, and so adds unity and thankfulness to his resume.

Judith is a person students go to when they think about their own calling or vocation, and she is fascinated by Brad's story and by the light the tournament shed on the school. "I think it felt good," she says, "because most days I come to work and there are students here in the Blue House and they say amazing things. They tell me an important story."

"These are really good students," she says. "I get to have really good conversations with them, and I see lightbulbs going on."

The games helped us think about how much we really do love all of our students. And all the national attention validated their choice to come to Butler, a liberal arts school with professional colleges in the middle of a city.

"I think about the world these students are going out into, and it's not easy," Judith says. "But if these young men and women are the ones, the world is in good hands. They come to this place knowing they're going to serve, that they want to volunteer. They assume service in some way. My generation, Generation X, didn't feel that."

Brad Stevens is of that generation; he's closer to the age of the current students. "Think of him at the Michigan game," she says. "This calm acceptance that it is what it is, that he believed in them no matter what.

"There was, in his demeanor, a transcendence of the victory."

Judith is particularly interested in how the experience of the tournament, and Brad's choices in particular, will help students think about vocation and about sacrifice and even failure.

She tells me about a student she talked with a lot in the past year, a young woman who came to Butler to dance. "Incredibly disciplined academically," Judith says. "Well organized. The dancers are very focused even when they know they're not going to be in a professional company.

"So here's this tiny little dancer. She had a bicycling accident a year ago, drove into a cord at dusk and it ripped her throat. So her dream is derailed. Now she's part of the community arts program, teaching in the city. She put on a mini *Nutcracker* for the Crystal Dehaan Center and has become an advocate for arts education.

"There's this incredible lightness of being in the students I see every day."

She describes another young woman student, a Pakistani American. For two years she was on the wait list for the physician's assistant program, but she didn't get in. In the long run it was cheaper for her to go ahead with a degree in religion than to wait. She's derailed but goes on to other things with the same tenacity.

She received the Peacemaker of the Year Award for starting the Muslim Student Association and meeting regularly with Hillel, the Jewish Student Association. "Ramadan and Passover overlapped, and it was her idea to get Hillel and the MSI together for a dinner to break the fast."

Lightness of being.

"This headscarf-wearing Muslim woman," Judith reflects. "She took Paul Valliere's mysticism course and read *The Pilgrim's Way*. She came to my office and said, I have to tell you about this book.

"She told me about a monk who would pray the Jesus Prayer every day so that God would become one with his own heartbeat. 'I started thinking about my own prayer,' she said. 'I walked to the car and said the Arabic prayer in the same way.'

"'Like him,' the young woman said, 'I want to feel that God is part of my beating heart.'"

"She's incredibly hardworking," Judith explains. And is not getting what she thinks she wants, a medical career.

"But that's how you find your vocation. Because you don't win the game or you don't get in the program you want. It's all part of the journey, that process of discernment. And maybe there's something in Brad Stevens's story. That's what history does for you. We've had too much divorce, but maybe in the family narrative there are clues to what we could be."


### THE DANCE

But if I'd only known how the king would fall
Hey who's to say you know I might have changed it all
And now I'm glad I didn't know
The way it all would end the way it all would go
Our lives are better left to chance I could have missed the pain
But I'd have had to miss the dance
Yes my life is better left to chance
I could have missed the pain but I'd have had to miss the dance
—GARTH BROOKS, "THE DANCE"

The week of the NCAA tournament the dancers in the Jordan College of Fine Arts were rehearsing for *Swan Lake,* a ballet about a princess who's bewitched and turns into a swan. It's all too much, this being one thing and being bewitched into another. How are you supposed to act? How are you supposed to feel?

The men's basketball team is in the fieldhouse doing drills, and the male dancers are in class, doing their leaps, jumps, and turns. It's been such a physical semester, and here when they're in class, the athleticism is more evident. Such height when they jump! Such control of their bodies in the air!

The athleticism of ballet. The aesthetics of basketball.

During a two-hour performance, according to dance instructor and choreographer Stephen Laurent, an "average corps de ballet dancer moves the equivalent of a piano a hundred feet in the air."

There are six weeks of rehearsals for every performance, three days a week for two and a half hours, all day on Saturday, and then the classes two or three times a day.

When the male dancers make a mistake, it's always when they land. Like ice skaters and gymnasts, like skiers and divers, they'll turn in the air in gorgeous spirals and then fall forward or bobble to the side when they come back down to earth.

"Why the landing?" I ask.

"Because," Stephen says, "The problem was there from the start, and they know it. They get up in the air and then they think about it and by then it's too late to make a change."

Is this like basketball? Yes, it's weirdly like basketball.

Because it all starts in the knees.

"It's the plié," Stephen says. Plié. French for bending of the knees.

Everything from a jump to a turn starts and ends with that movement.

Likewise, when a basketball player shoots a free throw, it starts in the knees. On defense, when you get into position, you bend the knees. When you get a rebound, before you jump. You bend the knees.

During the Duke game, my husband and our friend Garry said a sort of prayer together. They were both doing it, neither was aware the other was doing it, and it was one of the oddest, most primal things I've ever seen.

"Bend your knees," they were chanting, low, both to themselves and to the boys on the television screen. "Come on, boys," they were whispering. "Come on, son, remember. Slow down. Come on. Bend your knees."

It sounded as though they were trying to convey some wisdom that had been passed down from generations of fathers to sons and was repeated in shouts on the court, that had lodged itself in their heads as the whispers of their own fathers and that they were repeating as a mantra to the boys. *Bend your knees. Bend your knees.* Because when you get tense on a free throw, my husband explained, you aim without the essential bend. You think too much. Everything in ballet and basketball begins in that movement, that spring, those shock-absorbing powerful muscles that give both athletes and dancers the ability to fly and that have that terrible tendency to tear.

"There's an audience for that kind of excellence that there may not be for a student violinist or scientist," Duke's President Brodhead was quoted as saying. "But in a way the drive is continuous."

The drive.

Someone with a gift may have to be selfish in a game even when he's known for his humility, for passing the ball, for turning down four good shots for one great one. Or you may have to leave the institution that nurtured you, a community you love, because of the gift.

"When I was still dancing professionally," Laurent says, "I had to be extremely selfish, to baby my body. And then you get injuries—back, ankle, knees.

"When we cast our productions we always have understudies. We go to the bench. It's the depth of the bench that's important, knowing you have enough good dancers who can fill in if one gets an injury."

Of course there is no scoring in the arts.

Because the tournament turned the campus into a community and drew others in the community to it, there were many drawn into the hysteria who weren't basketball fans before.

Laurent was one of them, as were many of the dance majors before the big dance. Even they, Laurent said, were sucked into the hysteria.

"When I would see basketball scores before, it would feel almost absurd to me," he said. "Why do something if it only comes down to the final second? Why not just play that final second? Why do the rest?"

I get that, I say, I really do.

I enjoy watching basketball, but I feel the same way watching football. If it's tied at halftime, why did they bother beating each other up for all that time? Was it all filler during the commercials?

The difference between the two is that basketball, according to Laurent, is a functional aesthetic; the movements aren't for the sake of beauty only but are directed toward a goal, a literal one. Everything serves the purpose of those two or three points—all the blocking, receiving, shooting, all the passing. Ballet is a technical aesthetic: concerned with the beauty of the move, achieving the line. A bobble or fall might affect your career in the long run or affect a review, or you might be injured, but a mishap or a mistake erases a season or a game.

A basketball player can be as awkward as a colt, but if the ball goes in the basket, it doesn't matter.

But awkward movements usually don't result in the goal. Though when a player is awkward it increases tension in the spectator and thus surprise and delight, which are as much goals of any art as symmetry and fluidity. And basketball has its own geometric beauty that many basketball fans don't see in dance.

Perhaps it's in the training of the aesthetic sense, in the eye, in whether you yourself have ever participated in that particular dance.

In Indiana, at one time or another, we've all danced.

When a team makes it into the tournament, it's "*We're goin' to the dance, baby!*" Why dance?

There is something about the way each bracket looks on the announcement of the NCAA pairings (and it is "pairings," and the announcers talk about dance cards and dancing shoes) that has the perfect geometry, the elegance of Regency dance. The couples pair, they meet, they bow, they move up and down the floor in elaborate figures; they meet once again in a line and they change partners.

Perhaps this is true of other sports, but only in the college basketball tournament (which was based on the original Hoosier dance, the beloved one-class basketball tournament that I would, if I could have one wish at this very moment, bring back) does the analogy seem appropriate.

No one would call the Super Bowl "the dance."

And there is, there really is, a direct connection between dance and worship, between the body and the spirit. Dance is—and we've all felt it at some point in life while dancing—a way of communicating, of feeling communion, with the divine. The ecstatic motion of the whirling dervishes, for instance, is a way of transcending the ego, of forgetting the self. That ecstatic union is the basis of many mystical traditions.

Laurent explains that when humans first began to dance, everyone participated.

Then, slowly, it began to be clear that some were particularly talented.

The talented dancers became the high priests and priestesses.

Others became shamans, directors, coaches.

The rest of us became the audience.

We sit in our audience chairs with our audience remote controls and we express our pleasure or boredom with our thumbs.

But here's the thing. The main thing about Hoosier Hysteria in particular.

When Butler was winning, they were *us* and nothing else existed. They were part of our identity and we were dancing in the big dance. And we were dancing with everything that was good about ourselves intact. Everything.

"If you really deeply believe in the shamanic communication," Laurent said, "which at some level most of us do, then the priest, the dancers, have a power to reach the divine for us.

"It's the sense of awe.

"For a moment, at the end of *Swan Lake,* the audience in Clowes Hall felt it just as deeply."

I had heard Denise Levertov read on the Butler campus, and Wole Soyinka, and Nadine Gordimer. I knew about priests and priestesses. I knew the thrill of that religious sense and how it manifests itself in the arts. I've cried with shaking ridiculous sobs when I heard a young boy play *Rhapsody in Blue* on the piano. Nothing I love more in this world than a passionate geek, I told my friend Marianne.

But I've never felt it quite with this many people and all at once. Perhaps it's good that the arts are experienced in solitude or in relatively small groups. It was that experience magnified that lifted us out of the real and into the not-quite-real. It's good that both the arts and sporting events are bound by rules and by time. They bring joy and meaning. But that feeling is, like everything, double-sided. It the hysteria continues, if it asks you to leave your real life for good, or if it claims to be the center of all meaning, or begins to take away your sense of freedom rather than returning you to it, the hysteria of the crowd can turn demonic, religious ecstasy to agony, on a dime.

We felt it during the games, certainly, but even more in that oddly surreal time between the games when we were dancing in the studios and walking across campus in the particularly amazing green of the spring of 2010. It was electric. Ecstatic. It was at times frightening. It was some particularly powerful mojo.

"It's like the IU games of the 1980s," says Stephen, a Frenchman who's been in Indiana long enough to understand the fever. "Even the dancers wanted to leave class to watch."

Because we were knocking off all the number one seeds. One by one. We were in the dance.

## THE DANCERS

Alex Anglin, Garrett Butcher, Zach Hahn, Gordon Hayward, Matt Howard, Avery Jukes, Emerson Kampen, Grant Leiendecker, Shelvin Mack, Ronald Nored, Nick Rodgers, Andrew Smith, Chase Stigall, Shawn Vanzant, Willie Veasley.

If you close your eyes, you can still hear the announcers call their names from courtside: *Shel*vin *Mack! Matt How*ard. Willie *Veas*ley! *Gor*don *Hay*ward! *Shawn Vanzant!*

And Coach Brad Stevens. Matthew Graves. Terry Johnson. Micah Shrewsberry. Darnell Archey. Brad Collier.

Thank you.

## OTHER VOICES: ALMOST RELIGIOUS

### A BUTLER SENIOR

So here's what it was like for me the night we made it into the Elite Eight.

I was sitting with a group of people in an off-campus apartment. They all had their spots that they sat in for every single game. They were quite religious about it, always sitting in the exact same place.

Even me. I'm not a super big sports guy, but my heart was beating just by watching the players run around so much. It's so intense.

I transferred to Butler, was in the College of Business the first year. I'm from out of state, and I changed majors. I'm graduating with a degree in biology and music. I was busy and didn't pay that much attention to basketball my first two years.

But this year there was so much more at stake. And every single one of those last few games came down to the wire. We got by just barely, all the way to the championship.

The last few minutes of the Syracuse game were crucial. I just remember the clock hit zero and right away everyone just jumped up and started screaming: yelling at the TV, yelling at the air, yelling at each other. Hugging, high-fiving, running around. Everyone was on their cell phone.

The frenzy probably lasted for five minutes straight.

Then everyone was like "Let's go to campus!!"

So we ran out into the street! I don't think my friends even locked their door.

I just remember we ran around the corner onto 49th Street. You could see down the street. There were a ton of people running across my field of vision, and you could just hear a bunch of screaming.

So I just started running, and so did everyone else. It was a big field of energy.

We turned the corner onto campus, and it was this huge mosh pit sort of party going on. Somebody started playing music somewhere. It was really loud, and the whole thing became this huge dance party.

I'm not sure how long it lasted. We stayed there for probably twenty minutes and when we left it was still going strong.

At Butler you're in a group, like anywhere. Greeks hang around with Greeks, dancers with dancers. That kind of thing.

But this.

It was just kind of an ecstatic fever. Everyone was everyone's friend.

### BUTLER STAFF, RECREATION CENTER

We all have rituals. I know that I could have done whatever and it's not going to dictate the outcome of the game. But you feel like you're behind them, you're pulling for them if you do the same thing each time. We all wore the same clothes on Monday as we did on Saturday. All the tournament games I watched by myself at my house. I didn't want to go anywhere. My brother watched by himself at his house. My dad did too. Growing up, my dad wouldn't go anyplace, like a bar, to watch games on television. It's what we did. So that was my ritual until the final weekend. I didn't want to do anything else. I was almost religious about it.

Growing up and being born and raised in Indiana, and coming from a family that lives and breathes high school basketball, being at Butler is special just because of that.

I grew up in Peru, Indiana, home of the Tig-Arena. My father has been an eighth grade basketball coach for almost twenty-five years. I watch basketball differently from other sports. The game is so much a part of me. Growing up, it's all we talked about. I come from a small town. That was the thing to do.

And this tournament has given my son something similar. My favorite story from all of this is from my two-and-a-half-year-old. We were outside playing, and he got in his little car. He got in and said, "Daddy, I'm going to work." I asked him, "Grady, where do you work?" He said, "I work for Butler basketball!"

During basketball season, once a week everything else was forgotten.

Tig-Arena seats 1,500 people, and it's always full. It's old-fashioned, with seats all the way around. It's hot. It's loud. It's dimly lit and it smells of popcorn. It was just an awesome experience to go to the game there.

What made the game special in a small town, and here at Butler, is that you and the community know the players. We used to go to the same barbershop, the same doughnut shop. So you're cheering on your friends. If you're sitting next to a player in class and that night they're playing in a national championship game, that's huge. And when it happens you think to yourself that this is what it's all about. This is the way it should be.

A lot of this gets lost in big college ball now. A lot of those players are "one and done."

I went to a recreation directors' conference in Anaheim during the tournament. We wore our Butler apparel. It was unbelievable the number of people who came up to us, whether it was at the airport, conference attendees, hotel workers. A small school like this has become so respected nationally.

Being in this field I have a lot of colleagues across the country. I got a lot of e-mails, everyone saying they supported us, were rooting for us. It made you feel proud to work here. You don't get that from an everyday job.

But with the Final Four, it elevated it to a degree that's almost unimaginable. I'll probably never experience anything like that championship game again in my life. I took a good friend with me, and he described it best when he said it was epic.

I don't know what I'd do if I didn't have basketball. I still play two, three times a week, and the reason I play is for the love of the game.

It's almost religious.

## STUDENT ATHLETE I

In 1914 the most popular man in New Albany, Indiana, was a basketball coach as well as Spanish and physics teacher, recently a Rhodes scholar, who wore knickers and a flowing cape and spoke with a slight British accent. His name was Edwin Hubble.

Yes, that Edwin Hubble.

In 1914 he led his team to an undefeated season, and in mid-March "the train carrying the coach and his eight-member team, bolstered by forty dollars in community donations, pulled out of New Albany amid "a veritable roar of unrestrained enthusiasm," and headed for the state championship high school basketball tourney, where they came in third. (A third was possible then.)

A part of Indiana basketball tradition is the fact that Edwin Hubble was a coach in the Hoosier Final Four.

## BASKETBALL STARS

During the week before the NCAA Final Four, at times the dome in the planetarium was open, letting the telescope see the heavens. The dome is like the eye of God and it opens, always, mysteriously. "The Heavens Declare the Glory of God" is chiseled in the stone on the outside of the building, along with the date: 1954. You know that someone is inside watching something, paying attention to something that none of the rest of us can see because of the illusion of the atmosphere.

The first day of the summer session, I go to the planetarium and hear the voice of the astrophysicist from the planetarium's one classroom. The voice carries and magnifies in the odd acoustical space. It's one of those places you could whisper and someone three stories up could hear you. I'm sure the astrophysicist could tell me why.

While I'm waiting for the class to finish, I look around me. In between photos of galaxies and stars there's a poster describing the value of the liberal arts: "Think for yourself and act wisely and well in the world. Evaluate important themes that shape our understanding. Engage ourselves in the principles, purposes, and practice of public life. Discover the sweep of living systems, from microbe to biome."

Once a Butler physicist said that teaching physics was like being a curator in a vast and amazing museum. This is beautiful, is it not? Direct your attention here. Isn't it amazing, how it all works?

I watch and listen to the astrophysicist as he teaches. There are eleven students in the class, and two of them, Ronald Nored and the freshman Andrew Smith, are stars.

If the players miss a class, all of the players run laps. The players don't miss classes, not even in the summer. Not even in the summer after a championship season.

One of the stories Brad Stevens loves to tell, in fact, is about hearing an argument coming from the locker room. When he went in, he saw Gordon Hayward and Avery Jukes standing in front of the whiteboard. They had erased the X's and O's from practice and replaced them with a problem that had been on the morning's physics test. They were arguing about the answer.

"Lickliter, Matta, Collier, Stevens—they've all kept good track of the players," the astrophysicist will tell me. "The players understand that when they miss class for a game, they have to make up their work. When they first come to class, they say 'yes, sir' and 'no, sir.' I say call me professor, call me Brian, call me Dr. Murphy, but not sir.

"Veasley and Vanzant were both in my classes. They're really nice. And they remember you when they see you.

"They were in my classes a year or two ago. I wouldn't have known they were on the basketball team, and it wouldn't have meant much more to me than any student athlete. But they were the only ones who came in to my office hours on a regular basis. They asked if they didn't understand something. They asked for help.

"I've taught at a large state school, and the difference here is that the athletes are so much a part of the campus."

The planetarium is filled with spheres, of course. The stairway is circular, as is the entry. Clear plastic globes and photos of stars and planets and even the midcentury modern chandelier with its spherical lights, all Sputnik inspired. On the board in the planetarium classroom today there are sections of the spectrum and the triangular symbols of focused lenses, and there are notes:

Energy of a photon. Planck's constant. Absorption line, continuous spectrum, emission line spectrum.

He's doing red shifts, I think, and blue shifts and motion and orbits and speed and all of those things that have everything and nothing at all to do with basketball.

I want to know what they were doing in the planetarium during the tournament, whether the spirit reached even the physics students—the self-proclaimed and proud geeks and nerds with their publications and their full rides to graduate school at MIT and Yale and Columbia, their eyes on those spheres spinning much more rapidly and importantly than the one in Hinkle Fieldhouse.

The astrophysicist spins. It's one of Kepler's or Newton's or someone else's laws of motion, I think, that I notice it because I myself am so dang slow. Brian is a world-class biker; he never sleeps. How could he? He loves it, all of this, this furiously spinning world, all of it set so mysteriously in motion.

His office is a computer lab. "You have to see this," he says.

The curator, I think. And what is it?

He checks into his computer and there on the screen is another planetarium, much like this one. Except that in the background there are snow-covered mountains. He opens program upon program and suddenly he's inside the computer inside the planetarium, which is up on a mountain in the Andes, and he's checking the weather.

Apparently while the dancers were dancing and the writers were writing and the teachers were teaching and the basketball players were playing, the university was buying partial interest in a consortium that runs a telescope in the Andes.

"So I'm there now," Brian says. He's in the Andes. It's the first time he's seen snow in the background, and he's excited about it. "And I'm going to log in to the cameras, and I'm going to turn the lights on." He clicks a button and on the screen I see the lights go on.

The telescope in the Chilean computer is twenty-four inches, about two-thirds the size of the one at Butler, which was once the largest telescope in the world open to the general public. The consortium also owns a telescope in Houston. Between the three of them they can determine distances, work with the parallax and angles. Parallax. It's the way the Greeks, without telescopes, knew with some certainty the distance to the moon and the sun.

A telescope basically works like the eye, collecting light. "They're big light buckets," he says.

And so what do we do with these telescopes? We watch spinning spheres.

Two nights a week, he and his students are in charge of it. He gets them set up, tells them what he wants them to observe and capture, and then he goes home around midnight. They have his cell phone number, and they call him with questions or with emergencies. Last Saturday he went to bed around two AM and the students texted him at three.

An emergency is any change in the weather, the slightest chance of moisture. The students close the lid over the eye of the telescope to protect the lens, which if physically damaged could only be repaired by a visit from physicists hours away.

He shows me what the students have been photographing. It's a globular cluster of 500,000 stars called M14, gravity pulling all the stars toward the center so there's a milky mass of them almost touching, dancing, though the distance between each one is actually around ten light-years, like the distance between the sun and Pluto. Gravity is holding them up in space with the same pull that directs the spinning ball toward the hoop, the player back down to earth.

I hope, I say, since I'm all worried about the cuts in NASA funding and about asteroids heading our way and going undetected (I watch those movies) that the students are watching for asteroids. I'm glad to know that someone is paying this much attention to the night sky. I feel protected by them. I'm always glad to know that someone in some university or laboratory somewhere is looking at anything I can't see.

They are, primarily, looking for planets.

And this is an amazing fact to me. He tells me that the first planet in another galaxy was only discovered fifteen years ago.

Impossible, I'm thinking, and of course I'm thinking of *Star Trek*. My Butler students have been writing about weird planets that bear no relation to the ones we can actually see for far longer than that.

We can detect them, no problem, but actually seeing them, he says, is another matter entirely.

A student who's stayed behind after class to work on a lab comes in with a possible answer to a question. Brian looks at it. That one's just wrong, he says. It's physically impossible. He sends the student back down to the lab.

What I wouldn't give to teach something where I could say something with that much assurance. Who wouldn't? We live in the world of slippage.

During the tournament, Brian was interviewed by Joe Staysniak, on local radio station WIBC, along with Dan Dakich, former IU assistant coach and player. "'Well, Joe,' I said, 'I have two student athletes in upper-level astrophysics. One was all-state in women's tennis. At Butler 15 percent of the students are athletes.'"

Another media person, I think, looking for metaphors. And so what are the connections?

As analogies, the astrophysicist says, first of all. He tells me that gamma rays are really energetic, whereas infrared photons are less so. So Ping-Pong balls are more like gamma rays.

Or if you know a student is on the golf team, he says, you can talk about the conservation of angle momentum. Mass times velocity equals radius so that as the velocity goes up, the tighter the spin. This helps dancers, ice skaters, understand the spin. I tell the dancers that if they could compress themselves to a tiny pole they'd be spinning as fast as an atom.

And of course the entire universe, I say, is filled with spinning balls. Why spheres? I ask, and not, say, pyramids?

Why is there air? Bill Cosby asked in one of his monologues. "To fill up basketballs" was the answer.

The universe gravitates toward spheres because it's held together by gravity, he says.

Except for the things that are shaped like footballs, he adds. There are football-shaped galaxies called proleate galaxies. And there are oblate spheroids, he says, flattened objects like Gouda cheese. It depends, he says, on how the object is rotating.

He talks about his most amazing student from the past semester, a young woman named Kim who's going to Cambridge. She had an internship last year with the most honored American woman in astronomy, who wrote Kim a letter of recommendation.

Some of her classmates had 4.0s. She didn't. Anyone can memorize, he says, but not everyone has the perseverance to do research. There are students who go into a lab saying to themselves that they're not going to give up on a problem. They get to a brick wall and they don't stop. They go through it, over it, go to the lowest point and go under it. Kim's like that, he tells me.

As if on cue Spence comes back to the office for the fourth or fifth time. He still doesn't have the answer right. He's sent back to the lab.

Fifty percent of our students go on to graduate school, he says. In the long run, it's two-thirds.

Did he go to the games?

I watched them with the students in Hinkle, he says. On the giant television screens. Watching the cameras record the spinning spheres.

On the night of the Syracuse game, however, he had to attend a lecture. He followed the game on his iPhone while listening to the speaker.

The thing about this team . . . , he begins. I could tell he was still thinking about Kim, his student. One thing I noticed, he says, is that by the time they got to the finals I *expected* them to win. All season it was like they wouldn't accept anything less. They wouldn't give up, and you felt it.

And the last shot? I asked. Oh, the heartbreaking always-to-be-remembered one shot away from actually being the movie, repeating the myth—can you explain it in terms of physics?

From a physics point of view, he says, when you're fading away as Gordon was, it makes a difference in the velocity. You have two arcs, the one going forward and the one going down. And there's the parallax effect and the size of the object and the velocity and the arc. The human brain knows that. It can calculate that.

And so was he so, so very close because he was a math major, because of the physics? Was it a matter of calculations? Should we recruit all physics students, all math majors, who also happen to be good at hoops?

He laughs.

The human brain, he says, wires itself through trial and error.

It's wonderful, he explains, to have an athletic director and coach interested in something other than wins. You have to have a feel for it. You have to teach your legs. You have to teach the brain the rhythms. If you stop to observe yourself, you lose it.

You *have* to learn to become disciplined, and you have to have passion.

Earlier, when I overheard him in the classroom, Brian was talking about the planet, about carbon dioxide and volcanoes and the earth's spin. We're in a relatively warm period right now, he said. Warm periods usually don't last more than ten or twenty thousand years.

The $CO_2$ levels are 30 percent higher than any time in the last million years.

You were talking about global warming? I ask. How do you feel about our future, I ask, thinking beyond the two-week period, fourteen rotations of the earth, when Butler was the center of the world.

It's undeniable that something's going to happen, he says.

How do we know it's undeniable?

I tell my students that only about 10 percent of even the faculty on campus can give you evidence that the earth goes around the sun.

Why? Because they have no evidence.

And why should they? We accept these things without going back to the beginning. We accept them on faith. Except in the disciplines—of literature, of math, of science—when someone is always going back to the beginning and moving through the discipline to the latest discovery and then to the next and the next one.

Still. The first explicit evidence that the Earth goes around the sun was in the 1800s. But the Greeks knew the Earth was round. They knew the moon was four times smaller than the Earth. They knew the sun could rotate, and if the sun could rotate the Earth could rotate.

They knew this simply by observing things. They made predictions. They knew this by critical thinking.

There are facts, he says, outside thinking. Everything, for us, is critical thinking and perseverance.

Ninety-nine-point-nine percent of all species have gone extinct.

Depressing, right?

But in addition to their regular classes, two nights a week his students stay up all night running a telescope in the Andes. They take thousands of pictures of a galaxy. They go through each one of the images and determine the color of each star—red or blue or yellow or orange—and they adjust the pigments in the final image.

When Spence comes back to his office with another wrong answer, Brian tells him to try a different formula. He sends Spence back to the laboratory one more time. He's teaching him to think and to persevere.

It's what he teaches every day.

*The world is charged with the grandeur of God,* I think as I leave the planetarium. I have Hopkins inside of me because I had a teacher who loved Hopkins. *When I heard the learned astronomer,* I think, *when I sitting heard the learned astronomer where he lectured to much applause in the lecture room.*

And I follow Walt Whitman, whom I also have inside of me because of the same teacher, into the mystical night air. It's a false dichotomy, I think, and always has been. Scientists and artists and mystics and athletes all pay attention to one thing, the thing they love, whatever it may be.

Their secret? "It is every artist's secret," Willa wrote. "Passion. That is all. It is an open secret, and perfectly safe. Like heroism, it is inimitable in cheap materials."

The artist and the pioneer, the farmer and the scientist and the great coach, perhaps, are all distinguished by a particular combination of imagination and will, and they all give up a bit of their own lives in order to create something for the next generation.

Why?

Well, according to Cather it is so that "into all the little settlements of quiet people, tidings of what their boys and girls are doing in the world bring refreshment; bring to the old, memories, and to the young, dreams."

## PHYSICS

Her new hobby that spring was photography, and she had spent the morning at the library, looking through books of photographs taken with infrared filters. She was a physics major. Lenses, microscopes, glass domes, were all obsessions with her.

She stopped by a craft store, bought some congo blue and red plastic cellophane sheets, and cut them into cheap glasses. All that afternoon she held the plastic strips across her eyes and saw every tree throwing off that ghostly white light that would be there all around you every day if you weren't cursed with human eyes. She walked around with those lenses during the tournament, and she lent them to people. See that? That's the radiation that turns every tree into a flame, that frosty pink-white light that burns in this world. The world looked like it did in the infrared photos, and it was so mysterious and beautiful, that world. The fading stars. She went to sleep at night under the spell of it.

The sweet smell of lavender on her comforter, the sweet smell of the spring night, she said later. So much, she thought, that we don't notice in the rush of time.

## OTHER VOICES: RITUALS

### ADMISSIONS STAFF MEMBER

I have to confess, I've never been to a Butler basketball game. I've watched them on television. I've worked at Butler for three years, and two of my children are students here.

Once the tournament started, I felt like I didn't want to jinx them by doing anything I didn't usually do. I watched them in my usual spot, in my usual attire. When the tournament started I had been watching at home. Typically I would be in my sweats, casual and all. I have a recliner that I would sit in, and when it got too tense I would stand and leave the recliner because I couldn't stand to sit anymore.

The day of the game I always would rush home. There were announcements about viewing parties at Hinkle or meeting at bars, and it all sounded like a lot of fun, but I couldn't bring myself to do it. I had to be at home wearing my sweats and my Butler baseball cap. And of course we won, and I felt like I'd done my part.

During the Final Four game, I thought about inviting my daughter over for the game. But I decided no, it had to just be me there and the dog. We'd pulled them through this far. The day of the semifinals I had run some errands and I didn't want to be gone too long or get involved in anything else because I thought it might delay me from the start of the game. I thought I'd just watch a movie. I'm a big Tom Hanks fan, so I thought I'd watch *Apollo 13*. It's not exactly a sports movie, but it's about these guys working together as a team and accomplishing something. It ended at the appropriate time, and luckily we won. For the championship game, I rushed home and watched *Apollo 13* again, hoping it would help.

DAWG POUND MEMBER:

I always wore the same thing. My Butler Dawg Pound shirt, my blue and white Mardi Gras beads, my Butler socks and my hat: a basketball net.

The night after the Syracuse game it was pouring down rain, nine o'clock at night, absolutely pouring, and people were charging into the streets, screaming, hugging strangers, high-fiving. When we won, I jumped up and yelled. Didn't put on my coat, just ran to Jordan Hall to be part of the crowd. Hearing the roar from the campus, from the Greek houses, everyone screaming! People were going crazy. It was one of the happiest moments of my life.

After that, I watched all the games at home because I'd watched all the games at home. I didn't want to break my juju.

## CHANT

Are?
You?
A Bulldog?
Hell, yeah!

I'd love to do that cheer, says a woman who has never said a curse word in her life. It seems like so much fun.

## TIME DELAY

The spring of the 2010 NCAA men's basketball tournament, when Butler University made it to the Final Four, was the one where we were all switching our cable boxes and televisions to digital and only a few people really understood or cared how or why. The only differences we noticed were that we suddenly had to use two remote controls instead of one to turn the television off and that we had to get a box that will be, I'm sure, an odd reminder of this particular decade in the way that eight-track tape players remind people of the '80s.

The televisions were all supposed to become obsolete or end up in landfills or something, though most of us knew that wouldn't really happen. Still, it was a threat hanging over us.

The point is that nothing that happened live on TV that spring was quite instantaneous, so the celebrations came in waves.

It was a time delay.

The weekend we beat Syracuse and made it to the Elite Eight, many of us watched the game on television from other places. Some of us were watching from the Brownstone in Chicago, where men were crying at the end of the game. Some of us were at a bar in D.C. Some of us watched from hospital rooms, and some of us watched from fiftieth wedding anniversary celebrations and from baby showers. Some of us were in California or South Carolina and loved wearing our Butler shirts without anyone asking where Butler was. One of us was watching on a big screen at home and pacing the floor while talking to her daughter, who was in Tampa visiting a grad school, on a weekend R&R from Haiti.

The last few minutes of the game they watched together, talking on cell phones. Shelvin's at the free throw line, the daughter would say, and Shelvin would get fouled and go to the free throw line. I'm nervous! the mother said. He made it! the daughter said, and her mother told her friends that Shelvin made it right before he swooshes the ball in and makes it. We won! We're in the Elite Eight! the daughter screams right before the last few seconds tick away and her mother's house in Indianapolis erupts with shouts.

A sophomore who was watching it with friends in a dorm describes it this way: "I was watching the game where we got to the Final Four and the TV I was watching it on isn't HD. We won and the group I was with ran outside to celebrate, but everyone with HD got it a few seconds after us.

"Once we were downstairs *everyone* rushed out."

It was a weird time delay, but then it kicked in. "It was really exciting. People were screaming and yelling, and everyone you ran into that you knew, you were hugging and jumping around. And people were dancing. Even professors were celebrating. The provost showed up.

"We were all pushing to be in front of the TV cameras, cheesin' really hard."

Those televised games and the way we had our own communities and then rushed out into the larger, even giddier one. It happened around Butler, it happened in neighborhoods, it happened downtown.

During the Friday night semifinal game against Michigan State we noticed a different type of delay. That's the moment we became disconnected. "I really wasn't into watching anything in the beginning of the tournament," one student said. "I figured we'd be out by the first or second round.

"The most exciting game for me was when we won the game that got us into the Final Four. That seemed unreal. When I watched us play Michigan State, I really thought we had zero chance of winning. I still believe today that we should have lost that game, based on our poor performance. With the championship game, I refused to watch.

"I got so worked up watching Michigan State that I didn't want to go through that again. I could hear people's reactions outside my window, and that was enough for me."

*That seemed unreal.*

For everyone at Butler, the Kansas State game was the moment when the surreal kicked in.

Even Brad Stevens's wife, Tracy, back in the motel room getting her kids to bed and watching the end of the game on television, was reportedly staring at the wall when he got back to the room. "You're going to the Final Four," she said to him. "You made it."

## STUDENT ATHLETE II

The week after Butler made it to the Final Four, Ron Nored went to a professor for his advising appointment. Tournament time was, among other things, advising week.

Congratulations, Ronald, his adviser said.

Humility is what you get with Ronald, she said.

Ronald said thank you, then immediately got out his computer and opened several screens. He was thinking of taking this course in the fall, and that one, and he wanted to get his reading teacher license in addition to his subject license so what courses did he need, and what courses would be useful, whether he needed them or not?

His goal, the adviser said, is to teach at a rural school in Mississippi. That's what he was thinking about when he came to my office, not basketball. Or rather, that's what he was trying to think about. He was trying very hard.

Ronald Nored Jr. came by his drive for service honestly. His late father was a community activist and preacher in Birmingham, Alabama, a man who raised millions of dollars to revitalize a declining neighborhood.

"When I came to Birmingham to pastor Bethel A.M.E. Church in 1987," Ronald's father wrote in his autobiography, "Sandy Bottom was indeed a very tough neighborhood. Many very low-income senior citizens lived in the neighborhood, and they had to contend with transients, drug dealers and bootleggers . . . Lots were overgrown and filled with trash. The infrastructure was sorely inadequate. On rainy days, water covered the front yards due to poor sewage and drainage systems. There were no sidewalks, curbs or gutters."

Ronald's father died in 2003, at the age of forty-three. In an article on ESPN.com, sportswriter Mark Schlabach quotes Nored Jr. as saying, "I'm just trying to do half of what he did, and he did it in 43 years. I think if he saw one of his sons loving people and loving God, he would be happy."

Earlier, one of his education professors explained that Ronald had a major project due. I'll give you another few days, Ronald, she said to him. I know you're busy.

He e-mailed the project from his hotel room in Salt Lake City. He turned it in early.

What you see with Ronald, the professor said, is what you get in class.

## STUDENT ATHLETE III

Whenever the press mentioned Gordon Hayward and Matt Howard as student athletes, they'd talk about their math classes. It was amazing enough that these athletes went to class, but the fact that they were taking *math* classes, so it seemed to the journalists, was close to miraculous. The only reason I can see for this is that journalists and writers are often not good at math and therefore athletes should be worse.

Dr. Jon Sorenson is a professor in the department of mathematics and computer sciences, and Matt Howard was in his class that memorable spring semester of 2010.

Jon is from an academic family. His father was a math professor at Valparaiso whose research area was game theory. "I teach object-oriented programming and data structures in Java," he says.

We're sitting in Starbucks next to the campus bookstore. I'm hoping he can explain game theory to me. I know that game theory has nothing to do with basketball, but I'm mining for metaphors. Because reporters often joked about Gordon Hayward's class in game theory this semester, I think I might find some connection. Instead we talk about algorithms because that's Sorenson's passion.

"Imagine a program like PeopleSoft," he says. "Underneath the program are all these algorithms. I teach students the standard algorithms and how to utilize them."

An algorithm? He sees the blank look on my face. "The telephone book names are in alphabetical order," he explains. "Would it still have all the numbers if it weren't?"

"Yes," I say.

"Would it be easy to find them?"

"No," I say. "It wouldn't."

"Algorithms make it easy to find answers quickly, if you set them up right."

Like de-cluttering your house.

Matt Howard was studying algorithms this semester, and what I want to know now is how they might have been connected to his play.

"Shooting a basket into the hoop is like an artillery problem in the military," Sorenson says. "You fire a cannonball, compute the trajectory. A human brain is making all these tiny calculations. If the human body behaved perfectly every time, then you would hit a three-point shot every time.

"Another example is if you look at the way a defense is set up and in the offense you decide on a play to get someone open. To make a shot that's uncontested. There's a technique or an algorithm for that. The team that does that regularly will score a lot of points.

"You could view it as an optimization problem. Tall players at a basket will dunk. Percentages of three-points at the three-point line is a different percentage. A player who gets the ball a lot over the course of a game is more likely to score points. It's statistics."

Any sport uses statistics. In baseball there's no clock, so you can make a decision based on statistics. The season is 162 games long. If you're always making the right decisions, it will work out eventually.

Basketball coaches don't usually deal in statistics. The game goes too quickly, and there are so many variables. They usually don't have time. And statistics "can't take into consideration a 'hot hand,'" Sorenson says. "The fact that a player is just playing really well that day. You can't necessarily explain it mathematically."

Coach Stevens is really good, Sorenson says. He's creative, but he's also been quoted as saying he thinks about the game statistically, as a puzzle to be solved. As a coach, he thinks statistically.

So it's typical for a fan to second-guess him, the professor explains. "Let's get Zach Hahn in now!" you'll shout. If you're thinking statistically, you might not necessarily react to the moment. You might not see what the coach knows.

For a player it's not useless to understand the geometry, though it's next to useless if that's all you understand. "What helps a lot with students who have had math," he says, "is that they see the play as problem solving whereas other players might see it as personal. It's easier to be dispassionate. If you've had the ball stolen on the previous play, it might cause you to see the next play as personal. But the goal is to score a basket, as a team. The reason we won so many games is that we played well as a team. They passed when they needed to, no matter what their hearts told them. They used their brains."

He looks around the Starbucks. The campus has settled now into finals. "There was a certain power in those weeks. It's odd to say this, but probably some of the events in the American Revolution felt this way. Like Bunker Hill. You can imagine that all of New England felt like this.

"That's one of the reasons I think the coach insisted the players go on with their regular lives. In the class that Gordon was in, we had one guy who was in the Dawg Pound. He went to all the games. Some of the other students seemed puzzled by that at first.

"Gordon made the rap that went on YouTube and then went viral. The one that ended 'Too big, yo. Too big, yo.' One of the students brought it into class. We wanted normalcy in the classroom as much as possible. I think it helped that the students teased him."

## AWE

During the weeks of the tournament all six sophomore basketball players lived in Unit 1B in the Residential College, a two-story white stone building with sunglass-blue windows. Junior Megan Walker was the resident assistant in Unit 1.

"They'd come back from a game," she explained, "and I'd be like 'I just saw you guys on TV!' It was like watching my babies out there.

"It was shocking to see how down-to-earth they were through the whole experience. They never acted different, no matter what. They'd still come in and hang out and just want to talk. Having a couple of them in my room and hanging out, just being regular kids, talking about anything, that was nice."

She expected an onslaught of people trying to get into the unit, but it never happened. "I was ready to fight them off with a broomstick or something," she says, and explains that the whole building took extra precautions. They locked the doors earlier, kept an even closer watch.

The only thing that really changed is the way other students talked to the players. "I don't know why," she says, "but people are just more afraid to talk to them now, or have conversations with them. There are kids that are more awestruck."

## GORDON HAYWARD'S DECISION: ON VOCATION

COACH NORMAN DALE: You have special talent, a gift. Not the school's, not the townspeople's, not the team's, not Myra Fleener's, not mine. It's yours, to do with what you choose. Because that's what I believe, I can tell you this: I don't care if you play on this team or not.

MYRA FLEENER: Leave him alone, all right? He's a real special kid, and I have high hopes for him . . . I think if he works really hard, he can get an academic scholarship to Wabash College and can get out of this place.

COACH NORMAN DALE: Why, do you have something against this place?

—*HOOSIERS*

*We've had a good program for the past twelve years, and we've never had an NBA player. Our pros are doctors and lawyers.*

—SPORTS DIRECTOR JIM MCGRATH

In the final weeks of the semester, Coach Stevens announced he would stay at Butler, and Gordon Hayward announced he was deciding whether to jump to the NBA or stay in school. We felt sorry for Gordon. Feeling sorry is your default mode, my husband says. You're projecting. Gordon's default mode is that he has that sweet and mournful face. It's easy to project feelings onto it.

It was everyone's decision, though, his decision. It's all our decisions in a landlocked state, whether to be the one who stays or the one who goes.

But I passed him on the stairs in Jordan Hall, I say. He looked sad, and very alone.

He had to choose the NBA, one of my students said. He has to do what's best for him.

Do you think he's taking a lot of flak from other students?

He had to take his Facebook page down, my student said. Everyone was begging him to stay. Anytime anyone sees him, they ask him to stay. His mother wants him to stay, I think. His father wants him to go. But no one blames him for the decision he's making. We're just wanting him to give us the same ride again. But how could he do anything different?

But I just passed him on the stairs, my student said, and he looks sad to me.

He just signed with an agent last week, a professor says at the beginning of summer session. I have two basketball players in my class. It's a small class and they were talking about it. How could he turn down guaranteed millions? Doing something he loves, that he's been preparing to do all his life. How could anyone turn that down?

He stayed in class all semester. He took his finals. He registered for fall semester classes. It was a decision, not a given. There was some back and forth there.

There was a rumor the university would take out insurance on him, a Lloyds of London type of insurance like on Betty Grable's legs in the 1940s, something that would guarantee the $6 million if he stayed and was injured.

That was just a rumor. Against NCAA rules.

Could his parents take out a policy like that? Perhaps.

Brad Stevens and Gordon Hayward looked like father and son, or rather, like an older and slightly younger brother. Their reddish blond Scotch-Irish hair, their blue eyes. Same build, one just a bit stretched out. They were both calm, Gordon a bit shyer, more distant.

So when Stevens did what we all hoped he would do but were afraid wouldn't, when he decided to stay on as Butler's coach and not take millions to go someplace else, we hoped it was an omen. Why does it seem like an ethical choice to stay? What virtues are displayed here? Humility? Loyalty? Temperance? Charity? It seemed virtuous.

You could argue that it's branding, a better story if he doesn't leave. You could argue that if you wanted, whether conscious or not: the young church-going coach who quit a lucrative job at a corporation to volunteer as a coach, a young coach from a small school who takes the school to the national stage and then retains loyalty to that school, to the boys on that team. Cynicism doesn't believe in virtue.

The cynic says that if he left for a big school, he'd be just another sell-out and now he's got the Butler Way behind him. In terms of branding and dollars in the long run, he's probably better off signing that contract with Butler.

It's been a lousy few decades that way. We've all been made cynics. We all believe we're constantly being manipulated by everyone. It's "the decline of being into having," as Debord wrote, "and having into merely appearing." We're drugged, he wrote, by these spectacular images.

The two weeks when Butler University made it to the Final Four were not about any of that. It all happened too quickly. It was something else. Everything about the Seabiscuit moment that was the tournament this year was against cynicism, and so I'm going to say that I believe virtue is possible, that not everything is to make or improve the brand, and that I absolutely love the fact that Brad Stevens made the decision to stay. It feels so anticorporate, so against the grain. It seemed so Wendell Berry of him. It's a validation of those particular values.

And we were hoping Gordon would be able to resist the call, that there is something intrinsically virtuous about being as true to your school as you are to your girl. (One reason why he came to Butler in fact was to stay near his high school girlfriend, to his particular small-town Lutheran church, to his family. Again, that is part of Brad Stevens's narrative as well—his wife, the parents in Zionsville, college in Greencastle and the church the whole family attends on Indy's northside. A liberal Methodist church.)

There was a beautiful innocence to all of it. Not ignorance—a kind of naïveté. "We were all counting on being naïve," Brad Stevens said, "to carry us through."

And it did. "This was the first tangible evidence," one fan said, "that the things we believed to be true, against the current of everything in the culture, were actually true. That hard work is good, and loyalty to family, playing fairly."

The professional teams even became part of it. An ad in the *Indianapolis Star* placed by the Pacers, the Colts, and the Indians said: "We may be horses and cats and clowns but for one month we were all Dawgs."

We're used to professional athletes being jerks, getting paid tremendous amounts of money and taking it for granted. Even in colleges, this is true. "We've become cynical about college athletics too," a fan said. "Even sixth and seventh graders are on traveling teams, going to Los Vegas with their parents. The universities use athletes, the AAU takes young basketball kids, and parents think it's their ticket to the pros."

At Butler, athletes live on campus in the dorms. They weren't celebrities before they were heroes, and despite everything they never began acting like celebrities once they were heroes. This may change, but in the months after the tournament it was as though they were almost embarrassed by the attention.

And there's the spiritual aspect. Stevens is active in his church. The Sunday after the championship loss, the congregation at his church, St. Luke's United Methodist, gave him a four-minute standing ovation. When Gordon went to his church on Easter, the Sunday of the Final Four, that small Lutheran church in Brownsburg, he got a standing ovation as well.

Those are the things Gordon is giving up.

These are the things I'm sure his mother is afraid of him leaving behind.

His mother was too upset to speak to reporters the day Gordon announced he was going up for the draft. Gordon is a math and engineering major, an academic all-star with A's and B's in math and physics.

While the team won as a unit, it was clear that Gordon had NBA-level skills. He was the one the camera wanted to see emerging from his Friday morning math classes.

"The one-time skinny kid who nearly gave up basketball to focus on tennis early in high school is now projected to be a possible lottery pick," reporter Jeff Rabjohns wrote in the *Indianapolis Star*.

"It's been kind of surreal," Hayward said to a reporter the first day he worked out before NBA coaches, after his decision. "I really wasn't recruited in high school that much. To go from almost giving basketball up, being a smaller kid, to playing at Butler, then to coming here, it's been kind of weird."

He came out of nowhere, and no one had heard of him. It's a story made possible by the fact that he had a huge growth spurt in high school, going from five-foot-eleven to six-foot-eight between his freshman and senior years. "He's made himself into a superstar," Syracuse guard Andy Rautins said. "He's a stud, through and through."

In some sense, he will always be alone.

Is there anyone recently who went to school with this kind of academic distinction in the NBA or who actually went back to school and finished after playing?

That's a stumper, a fan says. A good Saturday morning radio trivia question. The ones I can think of, he says, are mostly foreign players. Manute Bol spoke several languages, and he's done all that good work in the Sudan. He's a good role model for Gordon.

Another guy, a player from England, who became a child psychologist.

But the NBA is to the old college basketball as the Olive Garden is, as Cebula has pointed out, to a small family-owned restaurant in Italy. It's a simulacrum of the original.

Butler basketball this year was, to all appearances, a throwback to an earlier innocence.

We're excited about the draft. We are. We love everything about you, Gordon. We loved the calm you projected during the tournament. We loved the way you played. We loved the way you represented us. We love the way your family attended all the games, the way you look like your mother and your sister. We love your tenacity and your dream. We love your smile, and more than anything we love your joy and we love your innocence. And maybe we're jealous because your heroes, once you've helped to make them heroes, are supposed to remain one of you. We want to be loved as much as you have been loved. We hope you make it.

"I'm going to buy his jersey," one student said, echoing many of her classmates' sentiments.

I'm just afraid for him, she said. I'm afraid that his life will be sitting on the end of the bench, accepting meaningless games, sitting on a private plane watching the stars play poker for thousands of dollars, heading to the strip clubs when they land. I can't stand to think of it.

He can go to the winter social any time, I say.

Oh no he can't, she says. He will have changed. He won't be in a group of us all wondering if we'll go to Qdoba after the dance.

It comes back, she says, to how do you keep score.

If it comes down to money, then there was no question what he should do. I mean, so much of life is about having enough of it, being able to take care of your family. Any logical person should tell him to go.

But if you keep score in other ways, then it is a debatable question. I wish him nothing but the best.

---

To those who understand the slightness of an American's traditions, the place of sports in his life, and New York City's need to make do with what it has (the stadium, for instance, is a nearly impossible place to watch football), the Yankee Stadium can be a heart-stopping, an awesomely imposing place. . . . And where I have been in Los Angeles's vast Coliseum and Chicago's monumental Soldiers' Field and am able to imagine it, I am yet unable to imagine a young man coming for the first time out of those dugouts at that moment just prior to kickoff when the stadium is all but bursting its great steel beams with people. I am incapable of imagining stepping out and craning my head upward at the roaring cliff of color, wondering whether it be all a dream which might at any moment come tumbling down, waking me to life's hard fact of famelessness. The stadium stays. The game proceeds.

—FRED EXLEY, *A FAN'S NOTES*

---

## THE CHAMPIONSHIP GAME

*We might call it a free activity standing quite consciously outside "ordinary" life as being "not serious" but at the same time absorbing the player intensely and utterly. It is an activity connected with no material interest, and no profit can be gained by it. It proceeds within its own*

*proper boundaries of time and space according to fixed rules and*
*in an orderly manner.*
—CULTURAL HISTORIAN JOHAN HUIZINGA, DEFINING "PLAY"

Watch the game again. Watch it slow. The game is such a dance, my friend
Geoff says, in ten dimensions, a million interconnected decisions.

As with a work of art, you will notice different things each time you watch
it.

The more you know about the sport, the more you see. It's like listening to
a symphony, Geoff says, and learning to hear the different instruments.

Nored and Mack rebound furiously. At one moment Nored reaches in and pulls
the ball out from a player a foot or more taller and immediately, fiercely, runs
toward the other end of the court. "It takes," Geoff says, "tremendous physical
courage to rebound." And look at them! They get hit and keep going.

They all accept their roles, and no one is ever merely an observer. Each
player performs. When you watch a professional game, you see the players
almost stop to follow the star who's following the ball. Here there's no one
on the floor who isn't doing something, even outside the spotlight of the ball
itself. Rewind the game! Everyone is an actor. It's like a play, where each extra
knows he needs to be doing something or responding to what's going on
because he's part of the story. There's always something for each individual
player to do, whether the ball is near or not. You've got to force your player to
defend you because otherwise he'll be free to go after the shooter, and when
your shooter isn't seven and a half feet tall with once-in-a-generation gifts,
you've got to help him out.

It's more like chess than any other sport, but it's happening so quickly.
What player A does affects what player E does, and the players are moving
around the board at rapid speed. Each player is responding the way he's been
taught to respond by drills, knowing the place and position of each teammate. The coach is watching the culmination of those drills and noting how
each one of ten players is moving: the position of the arm, the movement of
the ball from left to right hand, the creation of open spaces by the picks and
screens of the defense allowing the surprise, the wonder, the unexpected play
that creates a goal. Delight.

In slow motion you notice the dance moves even more. A player leaps in
the air and shifts the ball from one hand to another. Hayward, in particular,

is deft and creative. He gets a rebound, moves the ball from his left to right hand, and makes a lay-up, all while in the air.

He can get from the three-point line to a lay-up in one dribble.

Look at Hayward smile on that rebound! He's happy to be there!

The camera cuts to a shot of his mother, who looks exactly like him—red-haired and elfin—and she feels every shot, every move of her son on the court. Her son! My God, her son. But Gordon doesn't seem to have a care in the world. He is *playing*. It's play. She has given birth to a human being who plays on the surface of this earth, and who deems it a very good place to be. (How could we have forgotten?)

The joy on Hayward's face is unlike anything, just the pure smile as he goes onto the court. He smiles with his eyes. It's like watching your own son as he does whatever gave him the most joy as a child—running out the door on the first day of summer, the ecstatic glee of a landlocked boy playing in the waves on the beach—it's all in his face, all sincere and so deeply beautiful and innocent, slightly self-conscious and sweet. And if he had made that last shot it would have resonated through sports history throughout time. The joy of a young boy playing.

Matt Howard gets hit so hard, over and over, his head hitting the boards, hitting the goal post. As a center, his job is to get hit and to keep on going. He looks as clunky as a Labrador retriever, but he's far more agile than he seems. He feels the defender with his shoulders and rolls around him. He's always where he should be, and often where he should be is where you would least expect him. He passes the ball. He saves it, over and over again. His stride is incredibly long, like a track and field star. And over and over, he draws the foul. Each time, he's asked to play the biggest and tallest guy, and he's always the shorter one. His physical courage is more evident than anyone else's. He gets hit and gets right back up. Like boxing. It's in how you take the hit.

(I'm writing this during the NBA playoffs. In this morning's paper there's an article about how the Los Angeles Lakers are offering the players $50 for every charge they take in the finals. Ron Artest is quoted as saying "I don't even know how to take a charge. To get the charge, you have to fall. I'd rather not fall.")

Matt Howard is so loved. Who are you going to marry when you grow up? a mom asks her three-year-old girl, all dressed in a Butler cheerleading outfit. Matt Howard, she says. I'm going to marry Matt Howard.

It was Matt who grew the mustache before the tournament when the rest of his teammates chickened out, and then he had to keep it (no matter how silly) because they were winning. There was a Facebook site during the tournament called "Matt Howard's mustache has more fans than Duke!"

In the Michigan State game, he suffered that concussion and came right back for the finals.

Zach Hahn comes off the bench and scores three points! Like he's saying, *I don't need to dribble. I come off the bench and I'm ready. Put me in!*

But he's too small to defend against this team, and so the coach, puzzle solving, begins pulling Hahn in and out, working the players like a football coach. Defense, offense, working the time-outs. But this isn't the slow lumbering of the football players on and off the field. It's quick. And sometimes, if Butler misses after a possession, a player who isn't as strong on defense remains on the floor and Duke goes after him. We're gonna kill the weak thing, Geoff says. That's why it's a chess match.

And Vanzant ties the game at 16. All the players are in this game to win. Avery Jukes plays the best game of his career. After a time-out when the team is falling apart a bit, it's Avery who makes the three. He gets ten points off the bench in ten minutes.

There's Hayward, all by himself with three Duke players, getting the rebound and making the jump ball.

So many brilliant passes by Hahn. Look at him! He knows exactly where his teammates are—even when they're behind him. He throws the ball backwards, over his head, absolutely confident it will be caught. And it is!

The dancers are watching the move from the dance studio. The astronomers are watching this defiance of gravity. The men in their living rooms in their favorite sweaters, the mothers pacing the floors; the students in their dorm rooms or apartments, at Lucas Oil, at the Hinkle viewing party; the alums in the bars: Plump's Last Shot, in Binkley's, in Moe and Johnny's, all over Broadripple in Indianapolis, all over the world.

Watch the game again. Watch it just to watch the coach. With 5:47 left in the game Duke makes a three-point shot. Any other coach would scream and bully his team. Brad applauds the good play. Did you notice that? He's applauding. Rewind the game. There he is. And it was a beautiful thing to watch the way the two teams danced that particular possession.

It's so Zen-like, Brad Stevens's reaction. It is what it is. It's always been what it is and he watches it unfold. He chuckles when a player misses a free throw. Like a loving parent. Good boys. He rolls his eyes kindly. *Oh Shelvin. Oh Gordon. There you did it. You silly boy.*

As a coach or teacher, it's hard not to give in to the nervous excitement we're feeling as we watch the spectacle, to think that your job is not to torque people. As we watch, we can hardly breathe.

The calm. The Zen-like calm. When did we first notice it? Perhaps when we saw the players walking to and from classes, such an odd and unreal sight after seeing their intensity on the court. They were almost shy. They smiled. They radiated something mythical, though maybe it was only the projection of our own faith. And while the day of the championship game and the week before were glittery with an excitement that was almost too large, the excitement was a bubbling under the surface like an underground spring. Just enough. Not too much. It was an excitement constrained by limits, we knew, by the game itself and by the tournament which would end, allowing life to return to normal.

To what extent does he know? Geoff asks about Stevens. To what extent does he know about the calm that radiates from him? Is he conscious of the way his personality is producing excellence all around him? Or is it the soft touch of the natural? A gift.

Geoff plays in a faculty pickup game once a week and has for years. Sometimes they play in the West Gym in Hinkle Fieldhouse, but if it's available they play on the main floor. It's easier, Geoff says, on all our knees. They time the game so they play before the Bulldogs practice.

But during the season, he says, there was one time their game was tied at 99 to 99 and Brad Stevens came out to the floor, ready to start working with the team.

We're sorry, the middle-aged guys say to the coach. We'll leave right away.

But Stevens says, "No, you guys finish up!"

Can you imagine any other coach doing that? Geoff asks. Letting a bunch of old guys play on the floor? Or the kids who run out on the floor, after every home game is over, during the regular season?

Every institution is the lengthened shadow of an individual, Geoff says, quoting Emerson.

The ball goes back to Hayward. Hayward makes a lot of space for himself. That's where you see the individual creativity, not the consequence of a patterned team flow. Hayward can feel the defense. At one point he moves down the court and avoids the foul but the player doesn't move the way he wants him to and it's like "OK, now I'm gonna have to make you foul me," as though he's saying "If you'd been a better dancer, we could have lit up this floor together."

When Hayward passes off to Howard with a minute left in the game and Howard scores, you know with any other coach or any other team that would have been hard for Hayward. He's the star, the one who has a real shot at the NBA. With a coach who recruited players based only on individual athleticism, one whose livelihood and reputation rested upon being the mentor for, say, a LeBron James, that pass might not have happened. Humility. Unity. And the story of Milan and Bobby Plump's last shot, the story of the heroic individual who saves the day for his team and community, is so ingrained, in all of us that we expect Hayward to take those clutch shots. This pass, along with others like it, is one of the reasons we're still in the game.

Shelvin Mack's play is incredible; he's persistent and brave. It's so hard to overcome the size of Zubeck and the other Duke players. Mack is barely six-foot-three and Zubeck is six-foot-ten So Mack's signature move, the drive inside, delay in the air, and then release toward the basket, is batted away time after time by Duke's center.

Still, it was Mack who made seven three-pointers in the first round against UTEP. And in this game it's Mack's three-point shot at 14:06 that brings the team's spirit back.

Teamwork. You can tell. It's always about the next guy stepping up when Howard is in foul trouble, when Hayward's not dropping the ball in the basket. That tall freshman, Smith, is always ready when he's called off the bench. There's always somebody there waiting.

*One regiment gets beaten back but the next one is ready in its place. All the World War II veterans misty-eyed in Hinkle Fieldhouse, remembering. Is this what it was all about? The GI Bill veterans returning to Butler after the war, getting married, having children. My father was one of them. The pilot who flew his plane was only twenty-one. My father was eighteen. He was a tail gunner. He's in his eighties. We found out during the tournament that he has cancer. The calm radiated from the team to my father, I swear. He wears his Butler cap and jacket to the doctor appointments. At one time he was a boy like the boys on this floor. You have inoperable cancer, the doctor says. Butler beat Syracuse, was his response. This book is for him. I'm writing this for him.*

In the championship game the size difference is hard to overcome, and it's amazing, minute by minute, how close the score actually is. "It's like watching some chess grandmaster that could play the strong side or the weak side and still win."

"Be a great teammate," Coach Stevens said before the game. "Be accountable. Remember if you're accountable you'll not only attract that which you want but that which you are. Let's roll. Be Bulldogs."

Again, how calm.

Let's roll. Be Bulldogs.

The speed with which the offense reacts when Duke misses! They're aggressive. They don't even take a second to compose themselves. They're out like a shot.

This is crazy exciting! Geoff says. We're watching it as though we haven't seen it before.

My heart's still racing a little bit, my husband says, even though I know how it's going to end.

At the end Zubeck flagrantly fouls Howard, hooking his arm. But we have to watch the game several times before we're ready to call it flagrant. At first we just felt it. Call the foul! Call the foul! we yell at the screen. We watch it again. We watch it a third time. The game is so physical, so many fouls on every play. You have to say it was fairly, if at times imperfectly, officiated. But to what extent does the story of the Cinderella team that is not supposed to win, which we want to win, determine the way the game is seen while the game itself is being played? Geoff asks.

Two great coaches. Two great teams. Geoff heard the Duke coach being interviewed after the game. He had his player miss that second free throw because he wanted to increase the probability of winning. Butler was playing so well near the end, if it had gone into overtime he was afraid we would win.

Near the end, the television announcer says, "This is worthy of an NCAA championship."

And so, finally, what does that mean? It means that in his heart everyone had bought into the idea that Butler was the underdog and that the underdog wins or doesn't win with a final shot. "Is this going to be a Duke night?" they said before the game began. "Or a *Hoosiers* sequel?"

As though if Butler won it would have been a miracle.

This team was undefeated in regular season play. They were Horizon League champions. Nationally ranked for nineteen consecutive weeks. They had twenty-six regular season wins and were the only unbeaten conference champion in the NCAA Division 1. A basketball history that goes back to Tony

Hinkle and two national championships in the 1920s, a history the thread of which was dropped but then picked up again over a decade ago. Through recruiting from within, through a string of good coaches, through players like A.J. Graves and Mike Green and Darrin Fitzgerald, smaller Indiana players with heart, and through the support of a community. If Butler had won, it would not have been a miracle. It would not have required divine intervention or the replaying of a myth. It was not luck. It was invisibility. How well do you have to play before you're noticed? Ask a woman. The team, I'm here to tell you, was there all season. The team was always already there.

## ANOTHER VOICE: ALUM II

I was overcome with a sense of pride for my team. I stood there, looking down at this group of boys that had brought not just a stadium but the whole nation to its feet. And I couldn't contain my pride and happiness. It's a feeling that has lasted far longer than the disappointment of not raising that trophy.

## *CIVILWARLAND IN BAD DECLINE*

My graduate students have already turned the story of being the only class that met the day after the championship game (when all classes were canceled) into a story about being the only class that met on the day of, at the very *time* of, the championship game. Stories are an engine for meaning, whether we live them or read them, and I've lived through enough history now, seen how details get written down and then quoted and quoted again and again, that I know how certain tropes have their own power. The *Hoosiers* trope, for instance. The trope of the school that does things right and lifts the heart of a community. We tell certain stories because we need them.

For the record, classes were held on the Monday of the game but canceled for the day after. It was a day to celebrate the run, to readjust, to come back down to earth.

And for the record it wasn't always perfect weather during the tournament, though that's the way it exists in my memory. At times it rained. The day of the championship game there was a storm over Lucas Oil Stadium, a clash of fronts that produced (and I'm not making this up) a complete and stunning rainbow an hour before the tip-off.

But I will always remember the night of the day after the championship game. It was a warm evening, unseasonably so, and the air conditioning was not on in Jordan Hall. My class met around dusk and the windows in the seminar room were open. The sky was a lavender-blue, the last of the white petals were blowing in the third floor casement windows, and the wind was oddly from the east, the direction all cathedrals face.

What were the players doing? Sleeping, catching up on their other lives, catching their breath, as we all were. Going on. One of the players, freshman Andrew Smith, played basketball in his driveway all night after the game. "After they lost," his mother told my student Jordan Fischer in an interview later, "we all came home. We knew Andrew was on his way. There were about twelve or fifteen people here. We waited up for him. It was probably about one thirty or two AM. We hear the door open and he walks in. I go up to him and give him a hug. I asked him if he wanted to cry, and he said no. All the different cousins had their things to say to cheer him up. We got him laughing. Then somebody said something about shooting hoops. And he said, 'I'd shoot some hoops right now.' All the parents go to bed, and the kids drive down to Zionsville park and turn the lights on and played hoops on the courts there. Then of course the cops drove up and sent them all home, since the park had been closed since eleven PM. I just love that story. That Andrew was playing basketball just hours after losing that game."

That's a good story. We'd been studying stories all semester, and that was a good one.

We'd all been up late the night before. It was like waking up from an odd dream. So we kept the lights off as long as possible; the room was that dusky light that makes you not quite trust your eyes, and for the first time in weeks it was quiet in the building and outside, on the mall.

Now and then a student would walk by the classroom and look in. What were we doing there? What was he doing walking by? The faces were calm now, without that giddy helium look. Serious faces, on their way to the library to study. It was, perhaps, a relief as routine set in. Which was more real, the day of the game or the day after? The day after felt like a place you could stay and raise a family, where you could study for a test and complain about your allergies. Perhaps human beings aren't equipped to live all the time in glory.

I would say that we were happy that night, in a normal spring way. The third floor of Jordan Hall in the spring is like a treehouse. That night we were reading a collection of stories by George Saunders called *CivilWarLand in*

*Bad Decline,* a book that is proudly, in a late-twentieth-century pre-9/11 way, written completely without similes, with no attempt to get at the likeness of two things in an attempt to touch at mystery or transcendence.

Though the author does, and I think this is because of the lack of similes, include a lot of exclamation points.

CivilWarLand is a dystopian America where everything is an approximation of an ideal at-one-time America, all fake but with the illusion of verisimilitude, an illusion kept running by violence and corporate greed. We recognize this CivilWarLand. We recognize and fear its bad decline. In some way, we're even comfortable with it. The two student presenters are dressed that night in Civil War reenactment costumes in honor of the book. We're back in the world of irony, where we've all been living for more than a hundred years.

We're back in the world where even amateur basketball players are commodities, trying for the attention of Nike or Adidas, picked over like fruit at the market, being appraised as individuals for their potential in the marketplace. We're back in the world where in the sports pages we read that a local high school player and his entire family are moving to Newark, New Jersey, to play for a prep school. He has offers already from four Midwest colleges and his parents are hoping the increased exposure will attract some offers from Eastern Seaboard schools. He will play for the place that offers him the best deal. His loyalties will have nothing at all to do with family or community. That's just the way it is. And so our connection to the player will be an anxious one, knowing he'll leave at the better offer. The Colts, for instance, are called the Colts because of the horse-racing tradition in Maryland, where they came from. So who might they leave us for? Who plays for us? Who carries our burdens, who lifts our morale in this age? "America's business approach to sport," according to anthropologist Janet Lever, "is the exception rather than the rule."

We're back in the world where the Gulf of Mexico, a paradise, will be filled with oil because of corporate decisions. Bad decline, such bad decline. It's hard to live in that world without respite.

The tournament allowed us, Suzanne Fong said while it was still going on, to think on those things that are excellent and worthy of praise and, more importantly, to believe that sometimes, despite our best efforts to screw things up, such things can take us by surprise. If only for two weeks. And she quotes by heart:

Finally, beloved, whatever is true, whatever is honorable, whatever is pure, whatever is pleasing, whatever is commendable, if there is any excellence and if there is anything worthy of praise, think about these things.

## A BLESSING

A week after the tournament ended, a retired alum walks into the campus bookstore and looks through the T-shirt stock for new ones to add to his collection. He's been collecting T-shirts for five weeks now and wants to make sure he hasn't missed a new design.

Perhaps the championship Butler T-shirts are here somewhere, in a box in the back, and waiting? He's hoping that he'll step into the parallel universe where the last shot circles the rim and drops three points' worth of *in*, where the team that should have won has the trophy.

That shot! Gordon Hayward took the very last shot at the half-court line for three points.

If the aim had been .5 of a degree to the left, less than the width of a shoelace, the ball would have hit the backboard three inches to the left and it would have gone in! The alum read this online.

The width of a shoelace separated the national champion from the runner-up, so maybe the loss was all a dream he had.

The alum's team was, after all, so close to perfection, close to the fulfillment of what seemed like destiny. At some point it started feeling both miraculous and so predestined you could almost relax and watch it unfold like a movie you'd seen several times before. It was a kind of faith, really, one we gladly leapt into. Conference champions, a record thirty-three wins in the season, a twenty-five-game winning streak and the whole arc of Angelo Pizzo's movie *Hoosiers* going for us. The media mentioned that movie so often it became the template for what should have been. Bobby Plump = Jimmy Chitwood = Gordon Hayward. Milan = Hickory = Butler. Bobby Plump's last shot was made in Hinkle Fieldhouse. It was destined! The reel had started running, he'd seen the movie a million times, and he'd settled in for the joyful ride of the way it was supposed to be. It came down to the last second as it has been doing in his dreams eternally.

It came down to this moment, the one described so well by Joe Posnanski in *Sports Illustrated*:

The ball is in the air. And because the ball is in the air, anything is possible. Miracle? Heartbreak? Pandemonium? Silence? Yes. Anything. That's the beauty of a magical game like this, and also the pain. The basketball is in the air. If it misses, Duke wins one of the greatest championship games ever. And if it goes in (and it looks like it is going in), Butler wins the greatest game that has ever been played.

The basketball is in the air, a 45-foot shot that looks like it is going in, and Duke coach Mike Krzyzewski knows that if it goes in, the right team won. And he also knows that if it misses, the right team won, too. This is that kind of game. Both teams have played impossibly hard. Every player defended with every ounce of strength they had. Every player made a winning play—something, a rebound, a block, a devastating pick, a tough foul, a big shot, a good pass, a hard drive to the basket—that added a line or shade to this masterpiece. Duke wore white, and Butler wore dark blue (the opposite of the image they came into this game with), but they played so much the same—the same energy, the same violence, the same togetherness, the same purpose—that at some point they just seemed to mix together into this wonderful blend of gray.

The alum looks through the racks of basketball shirts until he convinces himself once again that it isn't here. The championship shirt. No matter how many times he's pictured the ball on the rim of the hoop going in and not out, pictured the chest-bumping and the cartwheels of the team that should have won, his own heart rising up into his throat; no matter how many times he's pictured Brad Stevens and the team cutting down the net in Lucas Oil, the whole city erupting in so much joy it probably, if he's honest, would have killed him—his wishing won't make it happen.

And that's all right. It really is. That moment of silence after Butler's loss was a beautiful thing in itself. A giant inhalation of breath, and everyone experiencing it as he did. Pizzo himself, the screenwriter himself, was at the game and, it's said, he turned to his only begotten son and told him to remember the moment because he would never in his life experience something this great again.

So the alum is constructing a shrine to the moment when all good and evil hung in the balance, when the world might have been filled with so much glory it would have signaled the Second Coming. It was like that paragraph Grantland Rice wrote about Notre Dame: *Outlined against a blue-gray Hoosier sky, the Four Horsemen rode again as 55,000 spectators peered down upon the bewildering panorama spread out upon the green plain below.*

Or maybe it was October sky? No matter. It was like that, only there were 70,000 people cheering for his Bulldogs at the game and millions more the world over.

He'd been a successful man, this alum. He'd graduated in '62. Or '68, depending on how you count, he said.

Every bit of his genetic material was Irish.

And for the Elite Eight weekend he hadn't even been in the country, but he had carried his Bulldog nature with him. "There I was in all my successful opulence," he said. "I'd taken my family to Turks and Caicos and we watched the game in a bar. When I got back there was a torrent of e-mails saying they'd seen me on television.

"It's like I had done something myself, as though I had something to do with this."

Why did it feel that way?

"When a member of your family does well," he said, "we're a community. It's 'we' and not 'I' then. The 'we' rises above all other considerations.

"When you see young men of the character, the decency, the ordinariness rising like cream to the top, it's almost a blessing.

"It's a sense," he said, "that all is right with the world."

He repeated the story from David Woods's book *The Butler Way,* about the basketball team losing a game in 2003 and afterward helping a janitor pick up the trash.

"It's stories like that," he said, "that epitomize this program. It's the decency, the we-ness. It's familial. It always has been.

"I have a friend, a doctor, who was on the '62 team. He's the only doctor I know that refuses to think about money.

"Butler tends to inspire the best in us.

"And Brad Stevens is a great guy. He goes to my church, St. Luke's United Methodist, and he won't let the team get away from him. He'll keep recruiting this type of player, student athletes.

"And if they aren't good students when they come, they will be when they leave."

Both his children and his grandchildren attended Butler. They watched the final game together on his TV. He moved back to Indiana when he retired in order to be near his family, who stayed in Indiana. He lives a block away from campus.

How did he respond to the loss?

He sat "in stunned silence for thirty seconds," he said, "maybe a minute," and then "overwhelming pride unstuck my voice."

The sound that came out was joyful. It was like the carillon playing "Back Home Again in Indiana." It was everything he'd ever believed in made real.

"This was," he said, "the most important thing that ever happened to me in my life.

"Next to when I met my bride and to the birth of my children, this was the most important thing.

"More important than my graduation.

"More important than my job.

"It was more important than my birth! Nothing in my life was better."

And the shrine? He sends me an e-mail a few weeks after I meet him:

*Dear Dr. Neville. The shrine is going well. I've finally got the box built for the paper goods/remembrances and a fine artist here in Indy, Tom Webster, is turning columns to mount on the box. On the top of the columns are bulldogs (soon to be powder coated in Butler Blue) upon which the ball shall rest. I'm not sure yet if I will enforce a genuflection before viewing or just silent reverence.*

For that one moment the end of the story hung in the balance.

## EPILOGUE
### *Brad Stevens Basketball Camp*

From where I'm sitting in Hinkle, after the madness has passed over, the goal really doesn't seem that high. Everything looks human again, less mythic.

It's the opening of the first Butler basketball camp since the tournament. Hundreds of children from kindergarten to fifth grade are sitting on the floor in the fieldhouse, and Coach Brad Stevens, fresh off appearances on *Letterman* and *Good Morning America*, from throwing out the first ball at the Cubs game, from talking on the phone with President Obama—Coach Brad Stevens is talking to these kids like you would want him to talk to your own children. "The most important thing," he says, "is that you have fun. And drink plenty of water."

He has them do the clap that preschool teachers do to keep attention. He says, "Get runnin' one"—they clap once. "Get runnin' two"—and they clap twice. This will be how all the coaches bring the children's attention back when it wanders.

Brad Stevens, who at age thirty-three has more basketball victories in his first three seasons than any coach in major college history, who is the youngest coach to take a team to the Final Four since Bobby Knight in 1973: you would forgive him if he skipped basketball camp this year. I mean, these are kids and they won't know the difference. A couple of the seniors who were on the team are here, and the assistant coaches. He could take a break, he could be calling up some endorsements, or he could be hanging out with stars in Los Angeles.

But no. He's here, in Hinkle Fieldhouse. He looks as young as his players. He has no entourage, and there are no cameras other than the ones held by a few mothers with preschool-age children and babies.

Coach Stevens tells the first graders where the restrooms are, and he reminds them not to turn toward the east end of the building when they exit the gym because there's construction going on. He reminds them *where* to put their backpacks. He reminds them to *remember* where they put their backpacks. He reminds them to remember to *take the backpacks home* at the end of the day. He doesn't raise his voice at the italicized words; it's more of a sense of the rhythm of the sentences. He reminds them again to stay hydrated and he reassures them. Some of the kids, after all, have worried parents who are leaving their precious children here and they're hovering around the edges of the courts for a while before they leave.

"The day will flow really smoothly," he says. Most of the kids pay attention. Some of them are looking around at the championship pennants hanging from the ceiling. Some of the younger ones look a little scared, but that won't last long.

Coach Stevens talks to them gently. He reminds them of the importance of teamwork. "If we're going to be the best," he says, "then let's be the best collection of individuals that works *together* in the country. Become a better basketball player this week, but most importantly become a better teammate."

"Respect other people," he says. "That's the one thing we can control."

And so the day begins flowing smoothly. Coach Stevens hands things over to Coach Graves, who gets the kids into groups according to the class they will be entering in the fall. School ended just last week, and they who understand how important it is to a child to be recognized by the rising class and not the one just left behind.

The first graders go to one point in the gym and then the second graders and so forth. They're asked to line up by height. This is something that kids can do quite easily. The tallest one knows he or she is the tallest and everyone accepts that he or she is tallest. To figure out who's next tallest and so on, the kids stand back to back and measure one another; it only takes a minute or two. You're taller or you're not. Lining up this way allows the teams to be as balanced as possible in size.

There are several coaches for each grade—players and assistant coaches from both the men's and women's teams—and each coach assigns the kids numbers out of sequence: 4, 3, 2, 1; 4, 2, 3, 1; 3, 2, 4, 1; 1, 2, 3, 4; 4, 1, 3, 2 . . . This keeps the children on their toes, keeps them from shuffling around in line and counting ahead.

GREAT TEAMS HAVE GREAT TEAMMATES is on the back of one of the T-shirts. I look at the children's shoes, at the coaches' shoes. Coach Stevens's shoes are Nikes on this day, but unlike a sponsored AAU event, the other coaches and the kids are wearing a refreshing mix of Adidas and Nikes and off-brands. There are Butler T-shirts on a lot of the kids, but just as many grade school shirts and shirts clearly brought back from family vacations and hand-me-downs from revered older brothers and sisters.

Now comes the organization part, and it's smooth as can be. Second grade! Four coaches hold up their hands and all the second grade "ones" move toward the coach holding up one finger. "So where were you during the championship game?" a second grader asks his new mentor. "On the bench," he says. "But here's Coach Willie. You can ask Coach Willie [Veasley] about the championship game!" And Willie, the shy one, pats the child's head. There's a lot of hair tousling, a lot of kindness between the coaches and the kids. There's so much kindness in the gym you want to tell someone about it. So I'm telling you.

Does everyone remember our team name? a coach asks.

Virginia! his team shouts.

And ours? the other coaches ask. Syracuse! Michigan State! Indiana! the kids shout.

Does everyone remember my name?

It's Andrew!

We're gonna be undefeated! their coach says.

The kids move in an organized way from Hinkle's West Gym to the outside, to the gym in the new recreation center.

Soon fifth grade boys and girls appear on the asphalt outside of Hinkle. Their blue and white Butler basketballs are popping in the air like bubbles as the kids practice passing to their teammates.

They've only been teammates for about a half an hour.

In the rec center gym, first and second graders play the game itself. Their shoes thunder in the space, and they count down from five to one. The buzzer goes off, and the children scream with delight.

In the West Gym of Hinkle, third and fourth graders work on fundamentals.

The coaches, some of them members of the most recognized sports team in the country only a few weeks ago, wait quietly for one group of kids to be passed off to them. They're still calm, soothingly calm. They're more like friendly tour guides or ushers than stars, not a bit of the attitude often associated with celebrity. It's such a relief. I can't tell you.

"Hey, Sam!" a fifth grader yells across the court, "isn't Connor the best middle school in the whole world?"

"No, Creekside is!" his friend answers with pride.

Coach Stevens's appearance at the beginning wasn't just an appearance. He moves between the West Gym, the rec center, and Hinkle. He smiles that slightly amused smile. He answers questions, gives encouragement, looks happy to be there. He's kind even when no one in the world is watching. And more than anything, he's calm. And so the camp runs smoothly.

It was the calm, as much as the joy, that we felt on campus. Where did it come from? "From Coach," according to player and camp coach Willie Veasley. "He leads, we follow," he told *USA Today* reporter David Leon Moore during the tournament. "When those big runs came, Coach called a timeout and said a few calm words. Then he said he believes in us, he loves us, and we're going to win the game."

The kids at camp today either watched the games with their parents and grandparents and friends on their home televisions or went to Hinkle to watch on the big screen. They're kids who went to the street fairs, who dressed in Butler blue and cheered. They're with their heroes, and they're learning the fundamentals. *Be the best group of individuals working together in the country. Attract not what you want but what you are.*

## AFTERWORD
### *What Do We Talk About*
### *When We Talk About Surreal?*

In this book I've often used the word "surreal," a word members of the Butler community often used during those crazy weeks of the tournament. The night Gordon Hayward was drafted by the Utah Jazz, in fact, when his twin sister was asked on national television what it had been like to live through the tournament, she said it had been surreal.

I've asked myself often what we meant by that. It never felt quite accurate. It's a small distinction, perhaps, but I think what we were trying to describe was an experience of the uncanny.

There's a word for "uncanny" in almost every culture, and in the early part of the twentieth century Freud attempted a definition that's had staying power. For Freud, the uncanny is, among other things, an experience of "the thing that was once familiar" and now is *not* so. Religious feeling is one of those "once familiar" things for many. What is this feeling? we wonder. And where did it come from?

The uncanny can also be the name for everything within the familiar that ought to have remained secret and suddenly isn't. It involves intellectual uncertainty, in particular doubts about whether an apparently animate being is really alive or, conversely, whether a lifeless object might not be in fact animate. Puppets and robots and dolls can present us with a feeling of the uncanny.

So what does this have to do with a basketball tournament?

When something you've secretly wished for seems to be coming true in a very big way, it can seem uncanny. Or when, as Victoria Nelson explains in her book *The Secret Life of Puppets*, "the distinction between imagination and reality is effaced—when a symbol takes on the full function of the thing it symbolizes or when something that appears as imaginary appears real" and causes you for one second to doubt an absolute standard of reality, you have that feeling of the uncanny.

The uncanny relies on—perhaps not faith in, but at least a gesture toward—a platonic worldview, to the belief that there is, as Nelson explains, "another, invisible world besides this one, that our world of the senses is ruled by this other world through signs and portents, that good and evil are physically embodied in our immediate environment."

We experience the uncanny when something in our lives brings that other world, those secret worlds, back into correspondence with the one we think we're living in, when the ordinary tables and chairs and combs and brushes of our lives suddenly seem to take on a symbolic aura or when a web of symbols combines into myth and an old story suddenly appears all around you and you feel as though you're walking through it. That uncanny dream world can be a nightmare, as in the case of 9/11, or it can be the fulfillment of a wish. In the case of the NCAA championship game, the archetypes were all in place: David and Goliath, Cinderella, the Miracle of Milan, Indiana, as repeated in every sports film ever written. And while the archetypes were worth noting, and were noted in article after article about the tournament, the thing that felt so deeply weird about being a student or faculty or staff member on the Butler University campus in 2010 was that we were *inside the myth*. It was like being caught inside someone else's delusional system. It was a giddy euphoric feeling, but ultimately we knew it wasn't the myth that was real. It just tempted us into believing that it was.

When someone congratulated us on something we ourselves hadn't done, or wanted to have a picture taken with a "real Butler person," we knew both how beautiful it was as well as how dangerous it could be to fall into the sleep-walker's dream. And I'm speaking here as a less-than-bit player, as someone who just happened to be there. I can't even imagine how difficult it is to hold on to any sense of human identity if you're at the center of something like this. You have to have someone who says to you "Go to class. Just go to class. Put one foot in front of the other."

Sports, as Stephen Laurent explained about the arts, can become the "unconscious wellspring of religious feeling," as sports anthropologist Janet Lever puts it. Their value comes in part from their ritualistic power to redeem us, to put us in touch with magic, a task sports inherited from religion. Religious feeling is uncanny almost by definition, and there are two parts to the feeling: the stimulus and the ultimate cause of the stimulus. Freud believed the feeling itself was real but the stimulus was imaginary, and he describes this best in *The Future of an Illusion*. Rudolph Otto, in *The Idea of the Holy*, asserted that the feeling of the uncanny when experienced through anything other than religion is "a low grade type of religious response to something real, to transcendental or numinous reality." In other words, the feeling is unreal but the stimulus is rock-solid.

While religious traditions and sports fandom may serve a similar purpose anthropologically—"that sense of identification with others who share the experience, the commitment to an overarching nonmaterialistic goal, communal rituals that produce a collection consciousness," as Lever writes in *Soccer Madness*—"devotion to one may offset the need for the other." In many parts of the world, for instance, it's women who go to church and men who go to the games.

Why else do sports give us that buzz? As Lever explains, there are many reasons. It stands outside the daily routine and offers excitement and drama through conflict: there are combatants and the outcome is uncertain. And unlike fiction or even "reality" television, sports action isn't scripted. "Each contest is unique, unrehearsed, and finite, and the resolution, when it comes, is clear-cut."

We need that structure. We need rituals with a beginning, middle, and end outside the chaos of our lives. Unlike war, whose metaphors we borrow to explain sport, sport is conflict that begins in an agreement to play and with certain rules. It begins in collaboration and a shared tradition. It's *play* conflict.

And while a game can be played in a way that reflects certain values-- teamwork over individuality, humility over arrogance, and so on--in the end a win doesn't validate a way of life any more than a loss refutes it. It simply, for a while, feels as though it does.

And so, from where I'm sitting in this empty fieldhouse after the madness has passed over and the gray has once again descended, I remember the *New York Times* reporter with his notebook taking down his impressions, the group of men (including Bobby Plump, aka Jimmy Chitwood) talking about the "day" outside the basketball office (where the secretary's desk is lit a neon blue). I remember the lines of families outside the spirit shop, wanting to purchase and then take a plastic bag of the spirit home with them. I remember the giddy innocent faces of the students. I remember the woman bringing her live dog into the fieldhouse in order to take its picture with the cement one. I remember the huge television screens set up on the hardwood floor, the "Go Dawgs" signs in every window, the wonderfully ecstatic electrifying energy of the tournament.

In the fieldhouse, women's basketball banners are on the south side, the men's on the north, carefully balanced. The banners hang from bars, like gymnasts. Behind the hoops there are life-size panoramic posters of basketball fans, their faces painted with blue stripes, the shirts of each fan drawn with stripes radiating from the heart, animal-like. Every mouth of every student on the poster is open.

Some mouths are dark holes like the void inside the basketball and some have a perfect netlike row of white teeth. The open mouths range from zeppelin shapes to lozenges, from lemons to avocados--all shapes of ovals. The students' hands are raised high in the air.

These students are caught not in a particularly joyful moment but in an anxious one. Their own fates are suspended as everything goes into the moment when the ball goes in or *does not go in* the basket.

Then, you know, the faces will change. Momentarily, unless it's the end of the game, from joy or to despair. It's not a state you could live in.

In the fieldhouse, there are seven windows facing east. The windows to the north and south and the similar large windows to the west are covered, almost perpetually, with blinds. The western light would be too hot for the place. The bluest sky is slightly muted by the old wavy glass, like all cathedral windows. Still, the light turns golden on the gray seating, lines of chartreuse light along the tops of the bleachers. The shaded windows on the north are tilted open for air. As the weather outside changes, the weather inside changes, finding its balance. It's an ordinary day in the fieldhouse. Children are practicing on the court. Next year, come March, the madness will begin again.

# Butler University President Bobby Fong's Speech to the Team after Their Loss in the Championship Game

In preparing for the celebration rally the day after the championship game, I wanted to say something to the players, who were still hurting over their loss. I wanted to put into perspective what they had done for themselves and the university. This is what I said:

We're gathered together to express our appreciation to you, the players and coaches responsible for this year's remarkable season. You've raised the ceiling of Butler basketball to unprecedented heights. Last night, you left everything on the floor in an epic championship game.

As competitors, you play to win. There's nothing we can say to assuage the pain of the loss; only time will do that. But as Coach Stevens did in the locker room last night, I do want to remind you of what you have gained this season.

You have forged a bond with one another that will never be broken. You've worked together to be a winning team, and you achieved that to a degree beyond any team in Butler basketball history. It's not simply about records; it's about being there for one another, knowing that each teammate could be trusted to play his role. As Shakespeare's Henry V said, you few, you happy few, you are a band of brothers. That bond you will have for all your days.

And beyond that special bond, you have cemented the community of your fellow students. While waiting for your return from Salt Lake City, I conversed with a student who told me this. An acquaintance of hers at Syracuse talked about "when Syracuse wins." She would talk about "when we won." And she realized that at Syracuse, sighting a basketball player was a rare event. At Butler, three of you were in her classes. She concluded, "I'm not just rooting for my team; I'm rooting for my friends." You are an integral part of the campus community. In reunions to come, you will return to friends beyond reckoning.

And beyond your fellow students, you have the gratitude of Butler friends and alumni around the world. Your feats on the court have provided respite to an alumnus in Iraq. Your supporters in New Zealand, in Europe, even on a ship at sea, found ways to follow your journey in this tournament. Matt White, in the last stages of Lou Gehrig's disease, asked to be with you in Indianapolis to root for you. As he gave you inspiration, so did you give him joy.

That in the midst of this week's pandemonium you still attended classes has become a byword of how excellence in athletics and excellence in academics are compatible. College presidents have written about how your example stands for all the schools that seek to do right by their students. Commentator Pat Forde wrote this morning, "But Butler wins, too. And the maligned sport of college basketball, a greasy enterprise in recent times, wins a renewed level of nobility. And every small school wins the license to dream Butler dreams."

And finally, you have permanently altered the profile of your university. [...] Going forward, far fewer people will ask, "In what state is Butler located?" Because of what you have done, Butler has become an example of academic and athletic excellence. Because of what you have done, in the years to come, many more students will aspire to come to Butler, some to be athletes, others to be artists, and scientists, and educators. Because of what you have done, more people will better appreciate achieving difficult things by doing the right thing, by doing them the Butler Way.

These are what you have achieved this season. These are the gifts you have given to us. To echo Winston Churchill, "Never was so much owed by so many to so few." For all these reasons, let all of us here today stand and applaud what you have done.

*April 6, 2010*

# THE SCORES, IN CASE YOU'VE FORGOTTEN!

FIRST ROUND: Butler 77, UTEP 59
HIGHLIGHT: Shelvin Mack's seven three-pointers, setting a career
    high with 25 points.

SECOND ROUND: Butler 54, Murray State 52
HIGHLIGHT: Ronald Nored's late three-point play.

SWEET 16: Butler 63, Syracuse 59
HIGHLIGHT: Butler's win over the No. 1 seed, holding the Orange
    scoreless over the final five minutes.

ELITE EIGHT: Butler 63, Kansas State 56
HIGHLIGHTS: Butler's advance to the Final Four and Brad
    Stevens's celebratory chest bump with freshman walk-on
    Emerson Kampen after the game. (And on campus, the
    sound of Gordon Hayward's rap playing over a public address
    system.)

FINAL FOUR: Butler 52, Michigan State 50
HIGHLIGHT: Butler wins despite shooting only 30 percent from
    the field, and it felt like destiny.

NATIONAL TITLE GAME: Duke 61, Butler 59
HIGHLIGHT: The half-court shot by Gordon Hayward that
    rimmed out at the buzzer and ended the crazy wonderful
    ride.

**SUSAN S. NEVILLE** is a native Hoosier and Professor of English and Creative Writing at Butler University. Her books include *Indiana Winter* (1994), *Falling Toward Grace: Images of Religion and Culture from the Heartland* (edited with J. Kent Calder) (1998), *Iconography: A Writer's Meditation* (2003), and *Sailing the Inland Sea* (2007), all with Indiana University Press. She is also on the faculty of the Warren Wilson Program for Writers in North Carolina.